THE EATING WELL

DESSERT

COOKBOOK

A Division of EW Communications L.P.

Box 1001, Ferry Road, Charlotte, Vermont 05445-1001

EATING WELL: The Magazine of Food & Health*, is a registered trademark of EW Communications L.P.
For subscription information, write to EATING WELL, P.O. Box 52919, Boulder, CO 80322-2919 or call (800) 678-0541.

Library of Congress Cataloging-in-Publication Data

The Eating well dessert cookbook: 150 recipes to bring dessert back into your life, from the magazine of food & health.
p.   cm.
Includes index.
ISBN 1-884943-09-8 (hardcover) — ISBN 1-884943-10-1 (softcover)
1. Desserts.   2. Low-fat diet—Recipes.   I. Eating well.
TX773.E32 1996   96-1772
641.8'6—dc20   CIP

Editorial Director: Scott Mowbray   **Editor:** Susan Stuck   **Managing Editor:** Wendy S. Ruopp
Recipe Editor: Susan Herr   **Test Kitchen Director:** Patsy Jamieson   **Nutrition Editor:** Elizabeth Hiser
Recipe Development & Analysis: Susanne Davis   **Additional Recipe Development:** Lisa Cherkasky   **Recipe Tester:** Beth-Ann Bove
Proofreaders: Euan Bear, Suzanne Seibel, Anne Treadwell   **Permissions:** David Grist

Design Director: Joannah Ralston   **Associate Art Director:** Elise Whittemore-Hill
Photographer: Matthew Klein   **Photography Stylist:** Kemper Hyers   **Food Stylist:** Rick Ellis

Front cover: Key Lime Pie (*recipe on page 38*)   **Back cover:** Carrot Cupcakes (*recipe on page 20*),
Cran-Strawberry Ice Pops (*recipe on page 164*), Lemon Squares (*recipe on page 132*)

Distributed by
Artisan, a Division of Workman Publishing
708 Broadway, New York, NY 10003

Printed and bound in Canada by
Metropole Litho Inc., Montreal, Quebec

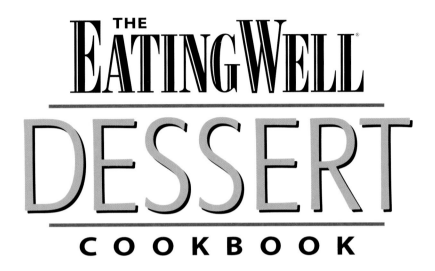

THE EATINGWELL DESSERT COOKBOOK

*150 Recipes
To Bring Dessert Back
Into Your Life*

from
The Magazine of Food & Health

EATINGWELL BOOKS

Raspberry Frozen Yogurt (*page 169*) & Sicilian Fig Cookies (*page 110*)

Chocolate-Cherry Bars (*page 100*)

CONTENTS

INTRODUCTION

It's time to bring dessert back into your life. No longer need dessert be too sweet, too rich or too heavy. The recipes in this diverse collection combine fresh flavors and healthful ingredients in a light, deft style that yields scrumptious results. Here you will find 150 treats that really do keep the EATING WELL mandate: to present our readers with a new approach to healthy cooking that fits the needs of their active lives.

In these pages you will find desserts for every occasion. Looking for a quick conclusion to a weeknight supper? Peach-Melon Frozen Yogurt or Brandied Nectarines can be made in under 15 minutes. Sweet delicacies for celebrations? Bake a Banana Spice Cake for Mom's birthday or a Café au Lait Cheesecake for Dad's. You have a choice of five harvest pies to grace a Thanksgiving table: the Mincemeat Tart has only three grams of fat per serving. Summer refreshments abound, from light and lemony confections to quick frozen fruit pops to nutritious (and portable) bars to pack into picnic baskets.

These desserts are not hard to make. The recipes are straightforward, having more to do with flavor than decoration. Still, skilled bakers will find they cannot wait to experiment with the innovative fat-cutting techniques, such as substituting dates for fat in a chocolate cake. Novice cooks intimidated by the words "pie crust" might want to start out with the easy Cranberry-Granola Blondies or Rum-Raisin Bread Pudding; neither takes more than 20 minutes to assemble. From there, they may feel confident to move on to the Lemon Cream Pie with its easy graham-cracker crust.

Some of these recipes have appeared in EATING WELL Magazine, many others have been developed expressly for this book. All have been tested and re-tested in the EATING WELL Test Kitchen, and that means one thing—these are recipes that work. You will find scores of tips throughout the book that give you a little extra information about a recipe. Some explain particular baking techniques, others help you select ingredients or suggest substitutions or variations.

Like all recipes from EATING WELL, these desserts are part of a diet built around fundamental, widely recognized healthy-eating guidelines: no more than 30 percent of calories in the overall diet should come from fat, and meals should include plenty of grains, vegetables and fruits. We not only pay attention to the amount of fat in a recipe, but also the source of fat, and strive to keep saturated fat to one-third of the total fat. No dessert in this book has more than 10 grams of fat per serving—not even the cheesecake! A nutritional analysis follows every recipe; it includes a breakdown of calories, protein, fat, saturated fat, carbohydrate, sodium and cholesterol for one serving. Nearly half of the recipes in this book are considered very low in fat—three grams or less per serving.

The desserts in this collection help you achieve another goal of healthy eating—to eat a variety of foods. At least 30 different types of fruit are used throughout the book: berries, peaches and plums are highlights of summer desserts; all manner of citrus fruits, apples, pears and dried fruits are part of cold-weather offerings.

So it's time to have a little fun and sit down to luscious desserts with a brightness and a lightness that will allow you and your family to enjoy dessert once again—with no trace of guilt and no end of satisfaction.

—Susan Stuck

◆ *For a list of the fat-free and very-low-fat recipes in this book, please turn to page 190.*

THE HEALTHY DESSERT KITCHEN

At EATING WELL, *we have found that by emphasizing fruits (fresh, frozen and dried),*
whole grains and low-fat or nonfat dairy products, dessert can be healthful and satisfying.
Here are some of the provisions and equipment we depend on to achieve delicious low-fat results:

DRY INGREDIENTS

BROWN SUGAR: Today's brown sugar is actually white sugar to which molasses has been added. Brown sugar adds moistness and deepens flavors, a plus for low-fat desserts. Light brown sugar is preferred when a strong molasses flavor is not desirable. Dark brown sugar is particularly good for deepening the flavor of chocolate.

CAKE FLOUR: A finely ground, soft white flour. Low in protein, it develops less gluten during mixing, so baked goods are more tender. An acceptable substitute can be made by replacing 2 tablespoons of flour with cornstarch for each cup of all-purpose white flour.

CORNMEAL: Adds an appealing crunchy texture to baked goods. If the package is labeled "stone-ground," the cornmeal includes the germ and some of the hull, so it is coarser and more nutritious. Store it in the freezer to keep the oils from going rancid.

DUTCH-PROCESS COCOA POWDER: Significantly lower in fat than chocolate, unsweetened cocoa powder is used to replace chocolate in dessert recipes. In Dutch-process cocoa, the natural acid has been neutralized, and the cocoa has a darker color and deeper flavor as a result. It is widely available at supermarkets or specialty-food stores.

INSTANT-DISSOLVING SUGAR: Also called superfine or bar sugar, this white sugar has a very fine granulation. Because it dissolves so quickly, it is excellent for instant frozen yogurts made in a food processor and for uncooked fruit sauces.

SEMOLINA OR SEMOLINA FLOUR: A golden, granular flour milled from the hearts of protein-rich durum wheat berries. Sometimes called pasta flour, because this is how it is most often used, it adds a pleasant grainy texture to desserts. Gourmet stores, Italian markets or large supermarkets will carry it.

WHOLE-WHEAT PASTRY FLOUR: A fine-textured, soft wheat flour that includes the wheat germ, giving it a higher fiber content than white flours. Look for it at health-food stores. Store in the freezer.

FATS & OILS

BUTTER: It is the only ingredient that will make baked goods taste truly buttery, but butter is too high in saturated fat to use in large quantity. The EATING WELL solution is to use a small amount of butter and magnify its flavor by heating until it turns a nutty brown. The recipes in this book were tested with and analyzed using unsalted butter.

CANOLA OIL: Pressed from rapeseed, this neutral-flavored vegetable oil is extremely low in saturated fats and quite high in monounsaturated fats. A must for low-fat cooking.

NONSTICK COOKING SPRAY: A mixture of oil and lecithin, this is a convenient and low-fat way to keep baked goods from sticking to the pan. It is available in aerosol and nonaerosol containers.

NUT OILS: Walnut and hazelnut oils are pressed from

toasted nuts. Buy nut oils in small bottles and store in the refrigerator, as they become rancid more quickly than other oils. When a recipe contains nuts, using a small amount of nut oil heightens the flavor. These oils are high in heart-healthy monounsaturated fats.

DAIRY & EGGS

BUTTERMILK: Tangy buttermilk, made by culturing skim milk with bacteria, is high in acid, helping to tenderize biscuits and cakes and keep them moist. If you don't have buttermilk on hand, substitute a mixture of half nonfat plain yogurt and half skim milk.

EGGS: All of the fat in an egg, about 6 grams, is found in the yolk. To reduce the fat in recipes, we cut back on the yolks and substitute additional egg whites. Because of the risk of salmonella contamination, adding raw meringue to a mousse or a filling is no longer recommended. To avoid that risk, our recipes use cooked meringues. Please note that all the recipes in this book were developed using large eggs.

EVAPORATED SKIM MILK: Made by evaporating nearly half of the water from fresh skim milk, this thick and slightly sweet canned milk product is a good replacement for cream in desserts where strong flavors will mask the slightly cooked flavor.

NONFAT AND LOW-FAT COTTAGE CHEESE: When the excess moisture is pressed out and the remaining curd is pureed in a food processor, this makes a great addition to cream cheese to expand its volume or a replacement for cream cheese in pastry doughs.

NONFAT AND LOW-FAT YOGURT: Like buttermilk, acidic yogurt helps tenderize baked goods and is a good replacement for sour cream. To replace cream cheese, make plain yogurt into yogurt cheese; use a brand without added starch, gum or gelatin and drain it overnight in the refrigerator in a strainer lined with cheesecloth. It will reduce in volume by about two-thirds.

SWEETENED CONDENSED MILK: Now available in both reduced-fat and nonfat forms, this is a canned mixture of sugar and milk from which about 60 percent of the water has been evaporated. It adds creaminess and body to desserts like custards and pie fillings.

FLAVOR ENHANCERS

CRYSTALLIZED GINGER: Also termed "candied," this is fresh ginger that has been cooked in a sugar syrup and dried. It lends a peppery pizzazz to desserts. Buy it at Asian markets or health-food stores, where it will be less expensive.

DRIED TART CHERRIES AND CRANBERRIES: Practically interchangeable, these two colorful fruits are wonderful in any number of desserts, helping to balance sweetness. They should be stored in an airtight container to keep them moist. Steep overly dry fruits in hot water for a few minutes to restore softness. Dried cranberries are widely available, but dried tart cherries may require a trip to a gourmet-food shop.

INSTANT ESPRESSO POWDER: More intense than instant coffee powder, a small amount of this dissolved in water or alcohol gives desserts a strong coffee flavor and intensifies the flavor of chocolate desserts. Find it at a large supermarket or specialty-food store.

SPICES: Because fat enhances flavor, baked goods with relatively small amounts of fat often need greater quantities of spices to prevent them from tasting flat. For best flavor, replace the spices on your shelf yearly.

SPIRITS & LIQUEURS: Alcohol adds a fat-free boost to flavors. Clear spirits distilled from fruits, such as kirsch (from cherries) or eau-de-vie de framboise (from raspberries), are effective in berry desserts. Calvados, an apple brandy from France, is a marvelous addition to apple confections. Liqueurs, such as Amaretto, with its almond flavor (actually made from peach pits), and orange-flavored Grand Marnier, add rich, mellow tones to a variety of recipes. Whenever possible, we have given a nonalcoholic alternative.

VANILLA AND ALMOND EXTRACTS: In low-fat desserts, the quality of extracts becomes even more important, because the flavor is more apparent. Avoid imitation extracts, which taste harsh and artificial, and buy only those labeled "pure."

VANILLA BEANS: They are expensive, but vanilla beans lend a complex flavor and fragrance to simple dishes, such as poached fruit, that cannot be matched by extract. Beans should be supple, not dried out. If the tiny seeds haven't been scraped out of the center, the bean can be reused two or three times.

ZEST: The term for the colored outside layer of a citrus peel. The oils in this layer are intensely flavored, making zest a flavorful addition to many desserts, especially fruit desserts. Use the small holes on a box grater to grate the zest, or a swivel-bladed peeler to remove it in long strips. Avoid the white "pith" just beneath, which is bitter.

BAKING PANS

The correct pan size is important to successful baking, but this can be confusing territory. If you have been baking for years, the size of the pans in your cupboard may be somewhat different from the pan we specify in the recipe or what is available in housewares stores. It is certainly possible to substitute a slightly different pan size, but try to keep the surface area close to the same. For instance, a good substitute for a 7-by-11-inch rectangular pan (with an area of 77 square inches) would be a 9-inch square pan (81 square inches).

Baking pans can be made of metal or glass, but cakes and bars bake slightly faster in glass pans. It is important to check baked goods often toward the end of the baking time, and to rely on directions in the recipe like "until it feels firm when lightly pressed in the center" or "until a skewer inserted in the center comes out clean" to determine when the dish is done.

Heavy baking sheets help prevent cookies from burning on the bottom. If you don't have one, stack two cookie sheets to solve the problem. Nonstick baking sheets are a wise investment.

SPECIAL EQUIPMENT

CHEESECLOTH: A loosely woven cotton cloth useful for fine straining or making pressed cottage cheese or yogurt cheese. Look for it at the supermarket or gourmet shops.

ICE CREAM MAKER: Look for the small countertop variety where you prefreeze the liquid-filled canister. They don't make a lot of ice cream, but are inexpensive and no-fuss.

INSTANT-READ THERMOMETER: Because it registers temperature so quickly, this tool is essential when making a meringue over simmering water, the only reliable way to destroy possible salmonella bacteria in an unbaked meringue.

NUTMEG GRATER OR GRINDER: While ground spices are usually fine if recently purchased, nutmeg is an exception. Always grate nutmeg fresh, as the flavor is quite different and far superior.

PARCHMENT PAPER: A strong paper, useful for lining baking sheets and cake pans to prevent sticking. While less expensive wax paper will often do instead, parchment is essential for cookies that tend to stick, such as meringues. Find it at kitchen-equipment shops.

SKEWERS: Bamboo skewers, the kind used for shish kebab, are indispensable for testing cakes and custards or to loosen cakes from fluted molds.

◆**HELPFUL TIPS**

Throughout the book, notes about ingredients, equipment and techniques are highlighted by the colored diamond.

UNFORGETTABLE CAKES

The gathering of family, friends or colleagues around the table as you cut into a cake—each person protesting that her slice is much too big—is the high point of many a celebration. Round and high—or even square and squat—cakes are used to mark important events in our lives. The cakes in this chapter are appropriate for occasions as merry as birthdays and as memorable as graduations. You will also find cakes for the more spontaneous celebrations. A superabundance of peaches in July? Celebrate it with a peach upside-

down cake. Like most of these light, delicious cakes, it uses fruits to spark bright, fresh flavors. And all are proof positive that a cake can be both festive and low in fat.

RICOTTA CHEESECAKE

Tart apricots and sweet golden raisins garnish this Italian specialty.
It can be served year-round but it is particularly appropriate at Easter.

CRUST

- 2½ tablespoons Grape-Nuts *or* Cheerios cereal
- 1 tablespoon walnuts
- 1 tablespoon sugar
- Pinch of ground cinnamon

FILLING

- 1 tablespoon pine nuts
- ⅓ cup golden raisins
- ⅓ cup dried apricots, diced
- ⅓ cup dark rum, kirsch *or* fresh orange juice
- 3 ounces reduced-fat cream cheese (6 tablespoons), softened
- ¾ cup sugar
- 16 ounces part-skim ricotta cheese (1¼ cups)
- ¼ cup nonfat plain yogurt
- ¼ cup all-purpose white flour
- 1 large egg
- 2 large egg whites
- 1 tablespoon fresh lemon juice
- 2 teaspoons grated lemon zest
- ⅛ teaspoon salt

TO MAKE CRUST:

Preheat oven to 325°F. Lightly oil an 8-inch springform pan or coat it with nonstick cooking spray. In a food processor, combine cereal, walnuts, sugar and cinnamon; process until fine crumbs form. Place the crumb mixture in the prepared pan; tilt and rotate the pan to coat the bottom and sides. Tap the pan on the counter to evenly distribute the crumbs. Set aside.

TO MAKE FILLING:

1. In a small dry skillet over low heat, stir pine nuts until lightly toasted, about 3 minutes. Transfer to a plate and set aside to cool.

2. In a small saucepan, combine raisins and apricots with rum, kirsch or juice; warm gently over low heat but do not boil. (*Alternatively, warm in a microwave oven.*) Let plump for about 20 minutes. Drain.

3. In a large mixing bowl, beat cream cheese with an electric mixer until smooth. Add sugar and beat until creamy. Add ricotta, yogurt, flour, egg, egg whites, lemon juice, lemon zest and salt, beating until thoroughly blended. (*Alternatively, mix ingredients in a food processor.*) Stir in the drained plumped fruit.

4. Transfer the batter to the prepared pan. Sprinkle with reserved pine nuts and bake for about 55 minutes, or until puffed at the edges but still slightly wobbly in the center. Turn off the oven and leave the cheesecake inside with the door closed for 30 minutes longer. Remove the cheesecake from the oven and let it cool completely on a wire rack. Remove the outer ring of the pan. Serve at room temperature or refrigerate, covered, for up to 2 days.

Serves 8.

270 calories per serving: 11 grams protein, 8 grams fat (5 grams saturated fat), 36 grams carbohydrate; 194 mg sodium; 47 mg cholesterol.

PEACH-BOURBON UPSIDE-DOWN CAKE

Bake this Southern-inspired, moist and fruity cake when peaches are plentiful—from late June through July.

1. Preheat oven to 350°F. Lightly oil a 9-inch round cake pan or coat it with nonstick cooking spray.

2. In a bowl, toss peaches with brown sugar, 1 tablespoon of the bourbon, if using, and cornstarch. Spoon the fruit into the prepared pan, arranging it in an even layer; set aside.

3. Spread pecans in a pie pan and bake for about 5 minutes, or until fragrant; let cool slightly. In a food processor, combine the pecans, flour, baking powder and salt; process until the pecans are ground to a fine meal.

4. In a mixing bowl, beat the 2 egg whites with an electric mixer until soft peaks form. Gradually beat in ⅓ cup of the sugar, continuing to beat until the egg whites are stiff and glossy; set aside. In a separate mixing bowl, beat the whole eggs with the remaining ⅓ cup sugar until thick and pale, about 5 minutes. Beat in the remaining 1 tablespoon of bourbon, if using, and vanilla. Whisk one-fourth of the reserved beaten egg whites into the whole-egg mixture. Sprinkle half of the flour mixture over the top and fold in with a rubber spatula just until blended. Fold in the remaining beaten whites, then the remaining flour mixture.

5. Spread the batter over the fruit in the pan. Bake for 35 to 45 minutes, or until the top springs back when lightly touched and a skewer inserted in the center comes out clean. Let cool in the pan for 5 minutes, then invert onto a serving plate, rearranging any stray fruit. Serve warm or at room temperature.

Serves 10.

180 calories per serving: 3 grams protein, 5 grams fat (1 gram saturated fat), 31 grams carbohydrate; 111 mg sodium; 43 mg cholesterol.

4	cups peeled and sliced fresh peaches (about 6 peaches)
2	tablespoons brown sugar
2	tablespoons bourbon (optional)
1	tablespoon cornstarch
½	cup pecan halves
⅔	cup sifted cake flour
1	teaspoon baking powder
¼	teaspoon salt
2	large egg whites
⅔	cup sugar
2	large eggs
1½	teaspoons pure vanilla extract

◆**PEELING PEACHES**

To remove the fuzzy skin from peaches, submerge them in boiling water for 20 seconds or so. Remove, dunk them in cold water, then slip off the skin.

A BOWL-OF-FRUIT CAKE

Celebrate summer's bounty with a simple cake ring that is filled to overflowing with seasonal fruits. The fruits listed here are suggestions; use what looks best at the market.

SPONGE CAKE RING

- 1   cup less 2 tablespoons unsifted cake flour
- 1   teaspoon baking soda
- 2   large eggs
- 2   large egg whites
- 1   cup sugar
- 2   teaspoons fresh lemon juice
- 2   teaspoons pure vanilla extract
- ⅓   cup skim milk, heated to about 150°F

FRUIT FILLING & GLAZE

- ½   cup sugar
- ¼   cup apricot brandy *or* fresh orange juice
- 2   teaspoons unsalted butter
- 4   cups pitted and sliced fresh nectarines (about 1½ pounds)
- 3   cups seedless green grapes (about 1 pound)
- 2   cups sweet cherries, pitted and halved (about 1 pound)

TO MAKE SPONGE CAKE RING:

1. Preheat oven to 350°F. Lightly oil an ovenproof ring mold with a 6- to 7-cup capacity or coat it with nonstick cooking spray. Dust the mold with flour, shaking out the excess.

2. Sift cake flour and baking powder into a bowl; set aside. In a mixing bowl, beat eggs and egg whites together with an electric mixer. Add sugar and beat on medium speed for 3 minutes, or until the mixture is pale and fluffy. On low speed, beat in lemon juice, vanilla and the reserved flour mixture just until the flour is incorporated. Beat in the hot milk.

3. Transfer the batter to the prepared mold. Bake for 22 to 25 minutes, or until a cake tester inserted in the cake comes out clean. Let cool in the pan for 5 minutes. Run a knife around the pan sides to loosen the cake. Invert onto a wire rack to cool while you prepare the filling and glaze.

TO PREPARE FRUIT FILLING AND GLAZE:

1. In a small saucepan, stir sugar and 1 cup water over medium-low heat until the sugar dissolves. Remove from the heat and stir in apricot brandy or orange juice. Pour half of the syrup into a small bowl, cover and set aside to cool.

2. Add butter to the syrup remaining in the saucepan, stirring until the butter has melted. Brush some of this glaze over the bottom and sides of the cake. Invert the cake onto a serving platter and brush the top of the cake with the remaining glaze. Cover and leave at room temperature until serving time.

◆**SPECIAL EQUIPMENT**
A ring mold is a deep, circular mold with a rounded bottom and a large center hole. You may use a 9-inch tube pan instead, but you will need to serve some of the fruit salad in a bowl alongside.

3. In a large bowl, combine fruit and the reserved cooled syrup. Cover and refrigerate for at least 1 hour or up to 3 hours. Just before serving, fill the center of the cake with the fruit filling. Spoon any syrup remaining in the bowl over the fruit.

Serves 10.

290 calories per serving: 5 grams protein, 3 grams fat (1 gram saturated fat), 62 grams carbohydrate; 120 mg sodium; 45 mg cholesterol.

A Bowl-of-Fruit Cake

BLUEBERRY TORTE

EATING WELL's *Test Kitchen Director Patsy Jamieson makes a trek to a cabin on the Maine coast every summer.*
She developed this cheesecake-like torte to celebrate the abundance of blueberries she finds there.

1½ cups all-purpose white
   flour

½ cup sugar

1½ teaspoons baking powder

½ teaspoon ground cinnamon

¼ teaspoon salt

¼ cup canola oil

2 large egg whites, lightly
   beaten

1 tablespoon melted butter

2 teaspoons pure vanilla
   extract

1 large egg

⅔ cup nonfat sweetened
   condensed milk

2 tablespoons cornstarch

1½ cups nonfat plain yogurt

   Grated zest of 1 lemon

3 cups fresh *or* frozen
   unsweetened (*not* thawed)
   blueberries

   Confectioners' sugar for
   dusting

1. Preheat oven to 300°F. Lightly oil a 9-inch springform pan or an 8-inch square cake pan or coat it with nonstick cooking spray.

2. In a mixing bowl, stir together flour, sugar, baking powder, cinnamon and salt with a fork. Add oil, egg whites, butter and 1 teaspoon of the vanilla; mix with a fork or your fingertips until well blended. Press into the bottom of the prepared pan.

3. In a mixing bowl, whisk together whole egg, condensed milk and cornstarch until smooth. Add yogurt and whisk until smooth. Blend in lemon zest and the remaining 1 teaspoon vanilla. Pour over the crust. Sprinkle blueberries evenly over the top.

4. Bake the torte for 1¼ to 1½ hours, or until the top is just set. (The center will quiver slightly when the pan is gently shaken.) Let cool in the pan on a wire rack. Run a knife around the inside of the pan to loosen the torte, then remove the outer ring of the pan. Serve warm or chilled, dusted with confectioners' sugar.

Serves 12.

240 calories per serving: 6 grams protein, 6 grams fat (1 gram saturated fat), 40 grams carbohydrate; 152 mg sodium; 23 mg cholesterol.

BLACKBERRY SKILLET CAKE

Enjoy a summer's day with an easy cake. Any blackberry variety is suitable here, from loganberries to marionberries to wild blackberries. Huckleberries are good too.

TO PREPARE FRUIT:

Lightly oil a 10-inch ovenproof skillet or coat it with nonstick cooking spray. Pour apple-juice concentrate into the skillet and add berries, distributing them evenly. To prevent the berries from floating to the top of the batter during baking, place the skillet and berries in the freezer while mixing the cake batter.

TO MAKE CAKE:

1. Preheat oven to 350°F. In a small bowl, stir together flour, baking powder and salt. In a mixing bowl, beat egg whites with an electric mixer at high speed until soft peaks form. Gradually add apple-juice concentrate, beating until stiff peaks form. Reduce the mixer speed to low and add milk, oil and vanilla, beating until well blended. With a rubber spatula, gently fold in the dry ingredients. Remove the skillet from the freezer and pour the batter over the berries.

2. Bake for 35 to 40 minutes, or until the top is golden and a skewer inserted in the center comes out clean. Let cool in the skillet on a wire rack for 10 to 15 minutes. Run a knife around the inside of the pan to loosen the cake and invert onto a serving plate. Let sit for a few minutes before removing the skillet, so the cake can absorb all the juices. Serve warm or at room temperature.

Serves 8.

265 calories per serving: 6 grams protein, 10 grams fat (1 gram saturated fat), 40 grams carbohydrate; 258 mg sodium; 0 mg cholesterol.

FRUIT

⅓ cup frozen apple-juice concentrate, thawed

3 cups blackberries, fresh or frozen

CAKE

1½ cups whole-wheat pastry flour (*see page 8*)

2 teaspoons baking powder

½ teaspoon salt

3 large egg whites

¾ cup frozen apple-juice concentrate, thawed

⅔ cup skim milk

⅓ cup canola oil

2 teaspoons pure vanilla extract

PLUM CAKE

A lightly spiced cake with a dramatic topping of glistening plums—it's perfect for a September birthday.

1   cup plus 2 tablespoons
    sugar

1½ pounds purple plums
    (about 8 medium plums)

1½ cups sifted cake flour

⅔   cup whole-wheat pastry
    flour (*see page 8*)

1½ teaspoons baking powder

½   teaspoon baking soda

1½ teaspoons ground
    cinnamon

½   teaspoon freshly grated
    nutmeg

½   teaspoon salt

⅔   cup nonfat plain yogurt

¼   cup canola oil

1   large egg

1   large egg white

1   teaspoon pure vanilla
    extract

½   cup red currant jelly

1. Preheat oven to 350°F. Line a 9-inch springform pan with foil, smoothing out the wrinkles. Lightly oil the foil or coat it with non-stick cooking spray. Sprinkle 2 tablespoons of the sugar in the bottom of the pan and set aside.

2. Halve plums lengthwise and remove the pits. Cut each half lengthwise into thin slices. Arrange circular rows of overlapping slices in the prepared pan; place any remaining slices in an even layer on top.

3. In a mixing bowl, stir together cake flour and whole-wheat flour, the remaining 1 cup sugar, baking powder, baking soda, cinnamon, nutmeg and salt. In another bowl, whisk together yogurt, oil, egg, egg white and vanilla until well combined. Stir the yogurt mixture into the dry ingredients with a rubber spatula just until blended.

4. Gently spoon the batter onto the plums, smoothing the top. Bake for 40 to 50 minutes, or until a skewer inserted in the center of the cake comes out clean.

5. Remove the outer ring of the springform pan, fold back the foil, and invert the cake onto a cake plate. Remove the pan bottom and foil.

6. In a small saucepan, whisk jelly over low heat until melted. Brush over the top of the warm cake. Serve warm or at room temperature.

Serves 10.

320 calories per serving: 5 grams protein, 7 grams fat (1 gram saturated fat), 62 grams carbohydrate; 223 mg sodium; 22 mg cholesterol.

◆**PICKING PLUMS**
Select slightly underripe plums for this cake—they hold their shape better while baking.

BANANA SPICE CAKE

As this bakes, it fills the whole house with a warm, spicy aroma that is particularly nice around the holidays. Delicious with Tropical Fruit Compote (page 59).

1. Preheat oven to 350°F. Lightly oil a large (12-cup) Bundt pan or coat it with nonstick cooking spray. Set aside.

2. Sift flour, baking powder, baking soda, cinnamon, nutmeg, allspice, ginger, cloves and salt together into a bowl; set aside.

3. In a small saucepan, melt butter over low heat. Cook, swirling the pan, until the butter turns a nutty brown, about 1 minute. Pour the butter into a small bowl and let cool slightly.

4. In a clean mixing bowl, beat egg whites with an electric mixer on low speed just until frothy. Add cream of tartar, increase the speed to medium and beat until soft peaks form. Gradually beat in ¾ cup of the sugar, 2 tablespoons at a time, just until firm peaks form; set meringue aside.

5. In a large mixing bowl, combine mashed bananas, oil, orange zest, vanilla, egg yolk, the reserved melted butter and the remaining 1 cup sugar; beat to combine. With the mixer on low speed, add the buttermilk and dry ingredients alternately in two additions each; beat just until blended. Add a heaping spoonful of the meringue and beat for just a few seconds to lighten the batter. By hand, fold the remaining meringue into the batter.

6. Pour the batter into the prepared pan and bake for 50 to 60 minutes, or until a skewer inserted in the center comes out clean. Cool in the pan on a wire rack for 10 minutes, then turn out onto the rack to cool completely. Before serving, dust the cake with confectioners' sugar and transfer to a cake plate.

Serves 16.

210 calories per serving: 3 grams protein, 6 grams fat (1 gram saturated fat), 39 grams carbohydrate; 249 mg sodium; 18 mg cholesterol.

2½	cups unsifted cake flour
2	teaspoons baking powder
2	teaspoons baking soda
2	teaspoons ground cinnamon
1	teaspoon freshly grated nutmeg
½	teaspoon ground allspice
½	teaspoon ground ginger
½	teaspoon ground cloves
½	teaspoon salt
2	tablespoons butter
3	large egg whites
¼	teaspoon cream of tartar
1¾	cups sugar
1	cup mashed very ripe bananas (2 large)
¼	cup canola oil
1	tablespoon grated orange zest
1½	teaspoons pure vanilla extract
1	large egg yolk
¾	cup buttermilk
	Confectioners' sugar for dusting

◆**BROWNING BUTTER**

Heating butter until it becomes fragrant and brown magically magnifies its flavor. Pour the browned butter immediately into a small bowl so it won't continue to darken from the heat of the pan.

CARROT CUPCAKES

Perfect for children's parties or office gatherings at any time of the year.

CUPCAKES

½	cup pitted prunes
1	8-ounce can crushed pineapple
1¼	cups sifted cake flour
1	teaspoon ground cinnamon
1	teaspoon baking powder
½	teaspoon baking soda
½	teaspoon salt
1	large egg
1	large egg white
¾	cup sugar
¼	cup canola oil
1	cup grated carrots

TO MAKE CUPCAKES:

1. Preheat oven to 325°F. Line 12 muffin cups with paper liners or lightly oil or coat the cups with nonstick cooking spray.

2. In a food processor, combine prunes with ¼ cup hot water and process until smooth; set aside. Drain pineapple in a strainer set over a small bowl, pressing firmly to extract most of the juice. Set the pineapple aside and reserve the juice for another use.

3. In a bowl, whisk together flour, cinnamon, baking powder, baking soda and salt. In a mixing bowl, whisk together egg, egg white, sugar, oil and the reserved prune puree. Add the dry ingredients to the egg mixture and stir with a rubber spatula until blended. Stir in carrots and the reserved pineapple.

4. Divide the batter among the prepared muffin cups, filling them about two-thirds full. Bake the cupcakes for 25 to 30 minutes, or until they spring back when lightly pressed in the center. Let the cupcakes sit in the pan for about 2 minutes, then transfer to a wire rack to cool before frosting.

Carrot Cupcakes

TO MAKE CREAM CHEESE FROSTING:

In a bowl, beat cream cheese, marshmallow creme and lemon juice with an electric mixer until smooth and creamy. Spread each cupcake with frosting and sprinkle with pecans, if using.

Makes 1 dozen cupcakes.

195 calories each: 3 grams protein, 7 grams fat (2 grams saturated fat), 31 grams carbohydrate; 206 mg sodium; 24 mg cholesterol.

CREAM CHEESE FROSTING

- 4 ounces reduced-fat cream cheese
- ½ cup marshmallow creme, such as Fluff
- ½ teaspoon fresh lemon juice
- 2 tablespoons chopped toasted pecans (optional)

GLAZED POPPY-SEED CAKE

A perennial favorite that looks dressy—with very little fuss.

TO MAKE CAKE:

1. Preheat oven to 375°F. Lightly oil a 6-cup or larger Bundt or tube pan or coat it with nonstick cooking spray. Sprinkle the pan with 2 or 3 spoonfuls of sugar, tapping out the excess.

2. In a mixing bowl, whisk together flour, poppy seeds, baking powder, baking soda and salt; set aside. In another bowl, whisk egg until frothy. Add sugar, sour cream, buttermilk, oil, lemon zest and vanilla and whisk until well combined. Stir in the dry ingredients just until moistened. Transfer the batter to the prepared pan, smoothing the top.

3. Bake for 20 to 30 minutes, or until the top springs back when lightly touched and a skewer inserted in the center comes out clean. Run a knife around the inside of the pan and turn the cake out onto a wire rack to cool completely.

TO MAKE GLAZE:

In a bowl, whisk together confectioners' sugar and enough of the lemon juice to make a smooth, thick glaze. Drizzle the glaze over the cake and let stand for a few minutes until set.

Serves 12.

260 calories per serving: 4 grams protein, 7 grams fat (2 grams saturated fat), 48 grams carbohydrate; 252 mg sodium; 24 mg cholesterol.

CAKE

- 2 cups all-purpose white flour
- 2 tablespoons poppy seeds
- 1½ teaspoons baking powder
- 1½ teaspoons baking soda
- ½ teaspoon salt
- 1 large egg
- 1¼ cups sugar
- ¾ cup reduced-fat sour cream
- ⅓ cup buttermilk
- 3 tablespoons canola oil
- 2 teaspoons grated lemon zest
- 1 teaspoon pure vanilla extract

GLAZE

- 1¼ cups confectioners' sugar
- 1½-2 tablespoons fresh lemon juice

GINGER-LEMON STACK CAKE

Three layers of an airy gingerbread with a tart lemon filling in between, this is a dependable, all-occasion cake.

LEMON FILLING

- ½ cup sugar
- 2 large eggs
- 2 large egg whites
- ⅓ cup fresh lemon juice
- 1 tablespoon grated lemon zest
- 2 tablespoons butter

GINGERBREAD LAYERS

- 1¾ cups sifted cake flour, plus extra for dusting pan
- ¾ cup sugar
- 1 teaspoon baking powder
- ½ teaspoon baking soda
- ½ teaspoon salt
- 1 tablespoon ground ginger
- 1 tablespoon ground cinnamon
- 1 teaspoon ground allspice
- ½ teaspoon freshly grated nutmeg
- ¾ cup buttermilk
- ½ cup dark molasses
- 3 large egg whites
- 3 tablespoons canola oil

  Lemon slices for garnish

TO MAKE LEMON FILLING:

Have a small bowl ready. In a heavy saucepan, thoroughly whisk together sugar, eggs, egg whites, lemon juice and lemon zest. Add butter and cook over low heat, whisking constantly, until the mixture has thickened and bubbled several times, about 5 minutes. (The lemon filling must be thoroughly thickened but not allowed to scramble.) Immediately transfer to the bowl. Place a piece of wax paper or plastic wrap directly on the surface to prevent a skin from forming and refrigerate until completely chilled.

TO MAKE GINGERBREAD LAYERS:

1. Preheat oven to 350°F. Lightly oil three nonstick 9-inch round cake pans or coat them with nonstick cooking spray; dust them with flour, tapping out the excess. (If the pans are not nonstick, line the bottoms with circles of parchment or wax paper and lightly oil or spray.)

2. Into a mixing bowl, sift flour, sugar, baking powder, baking soda, salt, ginger, cinnamon, allspice and nutmeg. In another bowl, whisk together buttermilk, molasses, egg whites and oil; whisk this mixture into the dry ingredients just until blended. Divide the batter among the three prepared pans, spreading it in thin, even layers.

3. Place the pans on the middle oven rack. (If they will not all fit, place one on the rack below, switching it with another pan midway through baking.) Bake for 12 to 15 minutes, or until the top springs back when lightly touched in the center; do not overbake. Let the cake layers cool in the pans for 3 minutes. Turn them out onto wire racks to cool completely, right-side up (removing the paper, if used).

TO ASSEMBLE CAKE:

Place a cake layer on a serving plate. Spread with half of the lemon filling. Repeat with a second cake layer and the remaining lemon filling. Top with the third cake layer. Garnish the top with lemon slices. (*The cake can be made up to 1 day in advance and stored in the refrigerator, covered with plastic wrap. Garnish just before serving.*)

Serves 12.

200 calories per serving: 4 grams protein, 7 grams fat (2 grams saturated fat), 33 grams carbohydrate; 222 mg sodium; 41 mg cholesterol.

BUTTERMILK POUND CAKE

Keep a cake in the freezer, to be thawed and dressed up with fresh fruit or sorbet for a last-minute celebration.

1. Preheat oven to 325°F. In a food processor or blender, puree drained pears. Transfer to a 9-by-13-inch or similar shallow baking dish and bake for 40 to 45 minutes, stirring occasionally, or until the puree is thick and reduced to 1 cup. (*Alternatively, stir the puree in a saucepan over medium-low heat until reduced to 1 cup, 10 to 15 minutes. This method is faster but messier and requires more attention.*) Transfer the puree to a mixing bowl and let cool completely.

2. Preheat oven to 350°F. Lightly oil a 10-inch tube pan or coat it with nonstick cooking spray.

3. In a small saucepan, melt butter over low heat. Cook, swirling the pan, until the butter turns a nutty brown, about 1 minute. Pour into a small bowl, stir in oil and set aside.

4. Sift cake flour, salt, baking powder and baking soda into a bowl and set aside. To the reserved pear puree, add 1½ cups of the sugar, buttermilk, vanilla, lemon zest, egg yolks and the butter-oil mixture and whisk until smooth. Add the dry ingredients in two additions, folding with a whisk just until blended.

5. In a clean mixing bowl, with clean beaters, beat the 4 egg whites until soft peaks form. While continuing to beat, slowly add the remaining ¼ cup sugar and beat until stiff, but not dry, peaks form.

6. With a rubber spatula, gently fold the beaten whites into the batter. Transfer the batter to the prepared pan. Bake for 40 to 45 minutes, or until a skewer inserted in the center comes out clean. Let cool in the pan for 5 minutes, then turn out onto a wire rack to cool, right-side up. (*The cake can be made in advance and stored in the freezer for up to 1 month.*)

Serves 16.

230 calories per serving: 4 grams protein, 4 grams fat (1 gram saturated fat), 45 grams carbohydrate; 227 mg sodium; 31 mg cholesterol.

2	16-ounce cans pears in light syrup, drained
2	tablespoons butter
2	tablespoons canola oil
3½	cups sifted cake flour
1	teaspoon salt
1	teaspoon baking powder
½	teaspoon baking soda
1¾	cups sugar
1	cup buttermilk
1	tablespoon pure vanilla extract
1	tablespoon grated lemon zest
2	large eggs, separated
2	large egg whites

◆**LOW-FAT BAKING TIP**

Fruit purees can fill in for fat in baking, but prune puree or apple butter is too assertive for some desserts. The delicate flavor of canned pears works beautifully in this pound cake; baking the puree in a shallow dish is a spatter-free way to thicken it.

ORANGE CHIFFON CAKE

This recipe makes a large cake, ideal for large gatherings. Serve it with sorbet or fresh figs and orange slices, as pictured below.

2¼ cups sifted cake flour

1½ cups sugar

1 tablespoon baking powder

¼ teaspoon salt

1 tablespoon grated orange zest

½ cup fresh orange juice

¼ cup fresh lemon juice

½ cup canola oil

¼ cup frozen orange-juice concentrate, thawed

2 teaspoons pure vanilla extract

2 large eggs

5 large egg whites

¼ teaspoon cream of tartar

1. Preheat oven to 325°F. Have ready a 10-inch angel food cake pan, preferably with a removable bottom, and a long-necked bottle.

2. Into a mixing bowl, sift flour, 1¼ cups of the sugar, baking powder and salt. Stir until well blended. Make a well in the center of the dry ingredients and add orange zest, orange juice, lemon juice, oil, orange-juice concentrate and vanilla; do not mix. Set aside.

3. Separate the two whole eggs, adding the yolks to the well of dry ingredients and putting the whites in another large bowl. Add the remaining 5 egg whites and cream of tartar to the second bowl. Beat the whites with an electric mixer on high speed until they form soft peaks; gradually beat in the remaining ¼ cup sugar and continue to beat until stiff, but not dry, peaks form.

4. Without washing the beaters, beat the reserved bowl of dry and wet ingredients together just until blended. With a rubber spatula, fold this mixture into the egg whites in three additions. Pour the batter into the ungreased pan, smoothing the top.

5. Bake for 60 to 70 minutes, or until the top springs back when

Orange Chiffon Cake

lightly touched in the center. Immediately invert the pan over a long-necked bottle to cool completely upside down.

6. Once the cake has cooled, set it upright. Run a knife around the inside of the pan and slip off the outer ring of the pan. Run a knife under the bottom of the cake to release it. Invert the cake, remove the pan bottom and set the cake on a serving plate.

Serves 16.

210 calories per serving: 3 grams protein, 8 grams fat (1 gram saturated fat), 33 grams carbohydrate; 121 mg sodium; 27 mg cholesterol.

◆ *Chiffon cakes cool upside down to keep them high and delicate, so have a bottle ready over which to invert the pan.*

DATE & WALNUT CAKE

Like many Greek and Middle Eastern sweets, this cake is infused with a honey syrup. The cake is made with semolina flour, which makes it moist and dense.

TO MAKE CAKE:

1. Preheat oven to 325°F. Lightly oil an 8-by-12-inch or 7-by-11-inch baking pan or coat it with nonstick cooking spray.

2. In a mixing bowl, stir together sugar and yogurt. Add semolina, dates, walnuts, orange zest and baking soda; stir until well combined. Spread the batter evenly in the prepared pan. Bake for 30 to 40 minutes, or until the top is golden and the cake is set in the center.

TO MAKE HONEY SYRUP AND FINISH CAKE:

While the cake is baking, combine sugar, orange juice, honey, lemon juice and cinnamon in a saucepan; bring to a simmer and cook over low heat for 4 minutes. When the cake comes out of the oven, cut it into 15 pieces. Spoon the hot syrup evenly over the top, getting some around the edges and into the cuts. Let the cake cool in the pan on a wire rack. Serve warm or at room temperature.

Serves 15.

170 calories per serving: 3 grams protein, 2 grams fat (0 grams saturated fat), 37 grams carbohydrate; 65 mg sodium; 0 mg cholesterol.

CAKE

¾ cup sugar

¾ cup nonfat plain yogurt

1½ cups semolina flour (*see page 8*)

¾ cup chopped dates

½ cup chopped walnuts

2 teaspoons grated orange zest

1 teaspoon baking soda

HONEY SYRUP

⅓ cup sugar

⅓ cup fresh orange juice

⅓ cup honey

1 tablespoon fresh lemon juice

¼ teaspoon ground cinnamon

TRIPLE GINGERBREAD

Fresh, candied and ground ginger make this the most gingery gingerbread ever. It is the perfect warmup after a wintry day's activities.

GINGERBREAD

1½ cups all-purpose white flour

½ cup packed light brown sugar

1¼ teaspoons baking soda

1 teaspoon ground ginger

1 teaspoon ground cinnamon

½ teaspoon ground mace

¼ teaspoon ground cloves

⅛ teaspoon salt

½ cup dark molasses

½ cup fresh orange juice

1 large egg

2 large egg whites

3 tablespoons canola oil

2 tablespoons finely chopped crystallized ginger (*see page 9*)

1 tablespoon grated fresh ginger

1 teaspoon pure vanilla extract

WARM CITRUS SAUCE

½ cup white sugar

1 tablespoon cornstarch

¾ cup fresh orange juice

¼ cup fresh lemon juice

1 teaspoon grated orange zest

1 teaspoon grated lemon zest

2 tablespoons dark rum (optional)

1½ teaspoons unsalted butter

TO MAKE GINGERBREAD:

1. Preheat oven to 350°F. Lightly oil an 8-inch square baking pan or coat it with nonstick cooking spray. Set aside.

2. In a mixing bowl, whisk together flour, brown sugar, baking soda, ground ginger, cinnamon, mace, cloves and salt. Break up any sugar clumps with your fingers.

3. In another mixing bowl, beat together molasses, orange juice, egg, egg whites, oil, crystallized and fresh gingers, and vanilla with an electric mixer on medium speed until smooth. Add the dry ingredients and mix on low speed just until blended. Transfer the batter to the prepared pan.

4. Bake for 30 minutes, or until a skewer inserted in the center comes out clean. Let cool in the pan on a wire rack for about 15 minutes.

TO MAKE SAUCE:

1. While the gingerbread is baking, whisk together white sugar and cornstarch in a saucepan. Whisk in citrus juices and zests. Cook over medium heat, whisking constantly, until the sauce thickens and boils. Cook, stirring, for 1 minute. Strain the sauce through a fine sieve into a bowl and whisk in rum, if using, and butter. (*The sauce can be made several days ahead and gently reheated at serving time.*)

2. To serve, remove the warm cake from the pan and cut into 9 squares. Serve warm with the sauce.

Serves 9.

295 calories per serving: 4 grams protein, 6 grams fat (1 gram saturated fat), 56 grams carbohydrate; 178 mg sodium; 25 mg cholesterol.

SWEDISH ALMOND CAKE

In Sweden this buttery cake is called Toska Tårta *and is served with afternoon coffee.*

TO MAKE CAKE:

1. Preheat oven to 350°F. Lightly oil a 9-inch round cake pan or coat it with nonstick cooking spray; set aside. Sift together flour, baking powder, baking soda and salt into a bowl; set aside.

2. In a food processor or blender, puree pears until smooth. Measure out ½ cup of the puree; keep the remainder for another use. In a mixing bowl, combine ½ cup of the sugar, butter, oil, vanilla, almond extract and the ½ cup pear puree. Whisk until well combined; set aside.

3. In a clean mixing bowl, beat egg whites with an electric mixer on low speed until frothy. Add cream of tartar and beat on medium-high speed until soft peaks form. Gradually add the remaining ¾ cup sugar and beat until firm peaks form. Set the meringue aside.

4. Add ¼ cup of the buttermilk to the reserved wet ingredients and beat with the mixer on low speed. Add half of the dry ingredients and beat on low speed until just combined. Repeat with the remaining buttermilk and flour. (Be careful not to overmix or the cake will be tough.)

5. With a rubber spatula, fold in the reserved meringue. Transfer the batter to the prepared cake pan. Bake for 25 to 30 minutes, or until a skewer inserted in the center comes out clean. Let the cake cool in the pan on a wire rack for 10 minutes.

TO MAKE CARAMEL-ALMOND TOPPING:

1. In a small saucepan, combine sugar with ¼ cup water. Bring to a simmer over low heat, stirring to dissolve the sugar. Increase the heat to medium and cook, without stirring, until the syrup turns a deep caramel, 4 to 7 minutes. Remove the pan from the heat and slowly add buttermilk. (The caramel will harden.) Return the caramel to low heat and simmer, stirring constantly, until the caramel dissolves. Stir in almonds and almond extract.

2. Place the cake, upside-down, on a serving platter. With a thin skewer, poke holes all over the top. Spoon the topping over the cake, spreading the almonds evenly and letting the caramel drip down the sides. Let the cake stand for about 1 hour before serving, to absorb the syrup.

Serves 12.

255 calories per serving: 4 grams protein, 7 grams fat (2 grams saturated fat), 47 grams carbohydrate; 237 mg sodium; 6 mg cholesterol.

1½ cups unsifted cake flour

1 teaspoon baking powder

1 teaspoon baking soda

½ teaspoon salt

1 16-ounce can pears in light syrup, drained

1¼ cups sugar

2 tablespoons butter, melted

2 tablespoons canola oil

1 teaspoon pure vanilla extract

½ teaspoon pure almond extract

3 large egg whites

¼ teaspoon cream of tartar

½ cup buttermilk

CARAMEL-ALMOND TOPPING

¾ cup sugar

⅓ cup buttermilk

½ cup sliced almonds

1 teaspoon pure almond extract

Italian Cornmeal Cake

ITALIAN CORNMEAL CAKE

Called polenta dolce *in Italian, this cake is not overly sweet. It is quite wonderful when served with fresh fruit.*

1. Preheat oven to 350°F. Lightly oil an 8-inch springform pan or deep 8-inch round cake pan or coat it with nonstick cooking spray. Dust it with flour, tapping out the excess.

2. In a small bowl, stir together flour and cornmeal; set aside. Separate egg yolks and whites into two mixing bowls. Beat the yolks with an electric mixer on low speed until blended; gradually beat in ½ cup of the sugar and continue beating on high speed until the yolks are thick and pale, about 3 minutes. Beat in lemon and orange zests and vanilla.

3. With clean beaters, beat the egg whites on low speed just until foamy; increase speed to high. When the whites begin to form soft peaks, gradually add the remaining ¼ cup sugar, beating until the whites are stiff and glossy. With a large rubber spatula, gently fold the whites into the beaten yolks. Then gently fold in the reserved dry in-gredients just until combined. Transfer the batter to the prepared pan, smoothing the top.

4. Bake for 25 to 30 minutes, or until the center is puffed and springs back when lightly pressed. Loosen the edges and unmold the cake onto a wire rack; let cool completely.

5. With a long serrated knife, cut the cake horizontally into two layers. Set the bottom layer on a serving plate and spread with orange mar-malade. Replace the top layer and dust with confectioners' sugar.

Serves 8.

220 calories per serving: 5 grams protein, 3 grams fat (1 gram saturated fat), 44 grams carbohydrate; 35 mg sodium; 107 mg cholesterol.

¾ cup all-purpose white flour

¼ cup yellow cornmeal, preferably stone-ground

4 large eggs, at room temperature

¾ cup sugar

1 teaspoon grated lemon zest

1 teaspoon grated orange zest

1 teaspoon pure vanilla extract

½ cup orange marmalade
Confectioners' sugar for dusting

♦**ZESTING**

The zest is the colored outside layer of a citrus peel. The oils in this layer are intensely flavored. When grating or peeling the zest, avoid the white pith just beneath, which is bitter.

CAFÉ AU LAIT CHEESECAKE

With its light coffee flavor and silken texture, this remarkable cheesecake is a perfect dinner-party finale—elegant, satisfying and (though no one will guess) low in fat.

CRUST

3 tablespoons Grape-Nuts *or* Shredded Wheat cereal

1 tablespoon walnuts

1 tablespoon sugar

FILLING

2½ tablespoons instant espresso coffee powder

2½ tablespoons coffee liqueur, such as Kahlúa *or* water

16 ounces nonfat cottage cheese (2 cups)

12 ounces reduced-fat sour cream (1⅓ cups)

12 ounces reduced-fat cream cheese (1½ cups), softened

1¼ cups granulated sugar

6 tablespoons all-purpose white flour

2 large eggs

2 large egg whites

1½ tablespoons unsweetened cocoa powder

¼ teaspoon salt

⅛ teaspoon ground cinnamon

TO MAKE CRUST:

Preheat oven to 300°F. Lightly oil a 9-inch springform pan or coat it with nonstick cooking spray. In a food processor, combine cereal, walnuts and sugar; process until fine crumbs form. Place the crumb mixture in the prepared pan; tilt and rotate the pan to coat the bottom and sides with crumbs. Tap the pan on the counter to evenly distribute the crumbs. Set aside.

TO MAKE FILLING:

1. In a small bowl, dissolve instant coffee powder in coffee liqueur or water and set aside. Place cottage cheese in a double layer of cheesecloth and gather the corners at the top; squeeze out as much liquid as possible. Place the pressed cottage cheese in a food processor and process until very smooth, about 2 minutes. Add sour cream, cream cheese, sugar, flour, eggs, egg whites, cocoa, salt, cinnamon and the coffee liqueur mixture; process until smooth.

2. Transfer the batter to the prepared pan and bake for about 1 hour, or until firm around the edges but still wobbly in the center. Turn off the oven and leave the cheesecake inside with the door closed for 30 minutes longer. Remove the cheesecake from the oven and let it cool completely on a wire rack. Remove the outer ring of the pan. Cover the cheesecake with plastic wrap that has been lightly sprayed with nonstick cooking spray. Refrigerate for at least 4 hours or up to 2 days.

Serves 16.

195 calories per serving: 8 grams protein, 8 grams fat (5 grams saturated fat), 22 grams carbohydrate; 159 mg sodium; 51 mg cholesterol.

◆**LOW-FAT BAKING TIP**

Nonfat cottage cheese can replace a lot of the usual high-fat cream cheese in a cheesecake, but it needs to have some of the water removed.

HEAVENLY PIES

W hen the crust is tender and the filling is fresh and sweet, a pie can be a little slice of paradise. But pie-baking seems to intimidate many cooks, which is a shame because, in the words of accomplished pie baker and cookbook author Lisa Cherkasky, "As long as a pie is homemade, it is good. Even if it doesn't come out picture perfect, people still love it."

Pies present a particular challenge for the low-fat baker, because a tender crust requires a certain amount of fat, and a two-crust pie, even if made with EATING WELL's reduced-fat crust, is a little too rich in fat for us. But an easy solution is to bake a one-crust pie, leaving it plain and unadorned or perhaps adding a streusel or meringue topping.

RHUBARB CUSTARD PIE

For the prettiest pie, choose rhubarb that has a deep fuchsia-red color.

CRUST

1	cup all-purpose white flour
1	tablespoon sugar
⅛	teaspoon salt
1	tablespoon butter
3	tablespoons canola oil

FILLING

¾	cup sugar
1	tablespoon butter, softened
1	large egg
2	large egg whites
¼	cup skim milk
1	teaspoon pure vanilla extract
1½	pounds rhubarb, trimmed and cut into ¼-inch pieces (5 cups)
2	tablespoons all-purpose white flour

MERINGUE

3	large egg whites
¼	teaspoon cream of tartar
½	cup sugar

♦ **WORKING WITH A LOW-FAT CRUST**

Because there is so little fat in Eating Well*'s pie crust, it would get too dry if it were rolled out on a floured surface. Instead, roll the dough between sheets of plastic wrap.*

TO MAKE CRUST:

1. Position oven rack at the lowest level; preheat to 375°F. Lightly oil a 9-inch glass pie pan or coat it with nonstick cooking spray.

2. In a bowl, stir together flour, sugar and salt. In a small saucepan, melt butter over low heat, swirling the pan, until the butter turns a nutty brown, about 30 seconds. Pour into a small bowl and let cool. Stir in oil. Using a fork, slowly stir the butter-oil mixture into the dry ingredients until the mixture is crumbly. Gradually stir in enough ice water (1 to 2 tablespoons) so that the dough will hold together. Press the dough into a flattened disk.

3. Place two sheets of plastic wrap on the work surface, overlapping them by 2 inches. Place the pastry in the center and cover with two more overlapping sheets of plastic wrap. With a rolling pin, roll the dough into a circle about 12 inches in diameter. Remove the top sheets and invert the dough over the prepared pie pan. Carefully peel away the remaining plastic wrap. Fold the edges under at the rim and crimp. Chill the pastry while you prepare the filling.

TO MAKE FILLING:

In a mixing bowl, beat together sugar and butter until fluffy. Beat in egg, egg whites, milk and vanilla until well blended. In another bowl, toss rhubarb with flour. Stir the rhubarb into the egg mixture. Turn the filling into the crust-lined pan, spreading evenly. Bake for about 1¼ hours, or until the filling is firm. Let cool to room temperature before topping with meringue.

TO MAKE MERINGUE:

1. Preheat oven to 375°F. In a large mixing bowl, beat egg whites with an electric mixer on medium speed until frothy. Add cream of tartar and beat on high speed just until soft peaks form. While continuing to beat egg whites, gradually add sugar. Beat until stiff and glossy.

2. Spread the meringue over the cooled pie, making sure it touches the edge of the crust all the way around. Bake for 12 to 15 minutes, or until the top is lightly browned. Let cool for 1 hour before serving.

Serves 8.

295 calories per serving: 6 grams protein, 9 grams fat (2.5 grams saturated fat), 50 grams carbohydrate; 113 mg sodium; 34 mg cholesterol.

TWO-BERRY PIE

Raspberries and blueberries unite in a chilled pie. The berry filling is quite nice on its own, served in parfait glasses. The crust is an easy graham-cracker crust that is pressed into the pie pan.

TO MAKE CRUST:

1. Preheat oven to 350°F. Lightly oil a 9-inch pie pan or coat it with nonstick cooking spray.

2. In a mixing bowl, whisk egg white until frothy. Add graham cracker crumbs, butter and oil and blend with a fork or your fingertips until thoroughly combined. Press the mixture in an even layer on the bottom and sides of the pie pan.

3. Bake for 10 minutes, or until lightly browned. (Do not be concerned if there are small cracks.) Cool on a wire rack.

TO MAKE FILLING:

1. In a 1½-quart saucepan, combine 1 cup of the blueberries, 1 cup of the raspberries, sugar, wine and lemon juice. Cook over low heat, mashing with the back of a spoon, for about 5 minutes, or until the sugar is dissolved. Remove from the heat.

2. In a small saucepan, sprinkle gelatin over ¼ cup water; let soften for about 3 minutes. Heat over low heat for 1 to 2 minutes, or until the gelatin is dissolved. Stir into the berry mixture. Gently stir in the remaining 1 cup blueberries, 1 cup raspberries and liqueur, if using. Pour into a heat-proof bowl and set it over a larger pan of ice water. Stir gently for about 5 minutes, or until the mixture thickens slightly. Pour into the prepared crust, cover and refrigerate until set, at least 5 hours or overnight.

Serves 10.

160 calories per serving: 2 grams protein, 5 grams fat (1 gram saturated fat), 27 grams carbohydrate, 1 gram alcohol; 66 mg sodium; 5 mg cholesterol.

CRUST

- 1 large egg white
- 1½ cups graham cracker crumbs (12 whole crackers) (*see tip on page 140*)
- 1½ tablespoons butter, melted
- 1½ tablespoons canola oil

FILLING

- 2 cups fresh *or* frozen unsweetened blueberries
- 2 cups fresh *or* frozen unsweetened raspberries
- ⅔ cup sugar
- ¼ cup dry white wine
- 2½ tablespoons fresh lemon juice
- 1 envelope unflavored gelatin (2 teaspoons)
- 2 tablespoons crème de cassis *or* Chambord liqueur (optional)

◆**INGREDIENT NOTE**

Look for "I.Q.F." berries, meaning individually quick-frozen, which can be measured out as needed.

Raspberry Angel Tartlets

RASPBERRY ANGEL TARTLETS

Individual meringue shells hold a tart lemon filling and a cloud of fresh berries.

TO MAKE MERINGUE SHELLS:

1. Preheat oven to 275°F. Lightly coat eight large (10-ounce) custard cups with nonstick cooking spray.

2. In a large bowl, beat egg whites and cream of tartar with an electric mixer on high speed until soft peaks form. Gradually beat in sugar and continue beating until the whites are thick and glossy, about 5 minutes. Beat in vanilla just until combined. Spread the meringue over the bottoms and slightly up the sides of the prepared cups. (The meringue will rise farther up the sides of the cups during baking, and sink in the center when refrigerated.) Bake for 45 minutes. Use a knife to loosen the shells but do not remove the shells from the cups. Refrigerate immediately.

TO MAKE LEMON FILLING:

Have a medium bowl ready. In a heavy saucepan, whisk sugar, eggs, egg whites, lemon juice and lemon zest until well combined. Add butter and cook over low heat, whisking constantly, until the mixture has thickened and bubbled several times, about 5 minutes (the filling must be thoroughly thickened but not allowed to scramble). Immediately transfer the filling to the bowl. Place a piece of plastic wrap directly on the surface to prevent a skin from forming and refrigerate until completely chilled, about 1 hour. (*The shells and filling can be made up to 1 day ahead and refrigerated separately until just before serving.*)

TO ASSEMBLE TARTLETS:

Spoon the chilled lemon filling into the tartlet shells and fill the centers with fresh raspberries. Dust lightly with confectioners' sugar.

Serves 8.

225 calories per serving: 5 grams protein, 4 grams fat (2 grams saturated fat), 45 grams carbohydrate; 87 mg sodium; 61 mg cholesterol.

MERINGUE SHELLS

- 4 large egg whites
- ¼ teaspoon cream of tartar
- 1 cup sugar
- 1 teaspoon pure vanilla extract

LEMON FILLING

- ½ cup sugar
- 2 large eggs
- 2 large egg whites
- 6 tablespoons fresh lemon juice
- 2 teaspoons grated lemon zest
- 2 tablespoons butter
- 4 cups fresh raspberries
  Confectioners' sugar for garnish

◆**BEATING EGG WHITES**

Always start with a very clean glass or metal bowl when beating egg whites, because even the tiniest bit of fat will significantly reduce their volume.

BUTTERMILK CUSTARD PIE

A Southern favorite, this pie is smooth, tangy and delicious.

CRUST

1	cup all-purpose white flour
1	tablespoon sugar
⅛	teaspoon salt
1	tablespoon butter
3	tablespoons canola oil

FILLING

¾	cup sugar
¼	cup all-purpose white flour
1	teaspoon cornstarch
½	teaspoon salt
2	large eggs
1	large egg white
2½	cups buttermilk
1	tablespoon fresh lemon juice
1	teaspoon pure vanilla extract
	Freshly grated nutmeg for sprinkling on top
1	cup fresh berries, such as blackberries, raspberries *or* sliced strawberries (optional)

◆**STRETCHING BUTTER**

To achieve a buttery taste in a reduced-fat pie crust, "stretch" a small amount of butter by cooking it until it turns light brown (not black) and gives off a nutty aroma.

TO MAKE CRUST:

1. In a medium bowl, stir together flour, sugar and salt. In a small saucepan, melt butter over low heat. Cook, swirling the pan, until the butter turns a nutty brown, about 30 seconds. Pour into a small bowl and let cool. Stir in oil. Using a fork, slowly stir the butter-oil mixture into the flour until the mixture is crumbly. Gradually stir in enough ice water (1 to 2 tablespoons) so that the dough will hold together. Press the dough into a flattened disk.

2. Place two overlapping lengths of plastic wrap on the work surface. Set the dough in the center and cover with two more sheets of plastic wrap. With a rolling pin, roll the dough into a circle about 12 inches in diameter. Remove the top sheets and invert the dough into a 9-inch pie pan. Remove the remaining wrap. Fold the edges under at the rim and crimp. Cover loosely with plastic wrap and refrigerate for 15 minutes.

3. Preheat oven to 375°F. Line the pastry shell with a piece of aluminum foil or parchment paper and fill with pie weights or dried beans. Bake for 15 minutes, remove weights and foil or paper and bake for 8 to 10 minutes longer, or until the crust is golden. Reduce oven temperature to 350°F. Cool the pie crust on a wire rack while you make the filling.

TO MAKE FILLING:

1. In a mixing bowl, whisk together sugar, flour, cornstarch and salt. In another bowl, whisk together eggs and egg white until frothy. Whisk in buttermilk, lemon juice and vanilla. Gradually whisk the liquids into the dry ingredients. Pour into the crust and sprinkle the top with grated nutmeg.

2. Cover the edges of the crust with aluminum foil and bake for 30 to 40 minutes, or until the pie is no longer wobbly in the center (do not use a knife to check for doneness or a crack will result). Cool on a wire rack for 15 minutes, and then in the refrigerator until completely cool, about 2 hours. Just before serving, arrange fresh berries around the edge of the pie, if desired.

Serves 8.

255 calories per serving: 7 grams protein, 9 grams fat (2 grams saturated fat), 39 grams carbohydrate; 285 mg sodium; 60 mg cholesterol.

BLUEBERRY STREUSEL PIE

A crunchy, lemony topping crowns this appealing summer dessert.

TO MAKE CRUST:

1. In a medium bowl, stir together flour, sugar and salt. In a small saucepan, melt butter over low heat. Cook, swirling the pan, until the butter turns a nutty brown, about 30 seconds. Pour into a small bowl and let cool. Stir in oil. Using a fork, slowly stir the butter-oil mixture into the flour until the mixture is crumbly. Gradually stir in enough ice water (1 to 2 tablespoons) so that the dough will hold together. Press the dough into a flattened disk.

2. Place two overlapping lengths of plastic wrap on the work surface. Set the dough in the center and cover with two more sheets of plastic wrap. With a rolling pin, roll the dough into a circle about 12 inches in diameter. Remove the top sheets and invert the dough into a 9-inch pie pan. Gently press the dough into the bottom of the pie pan. Remove the remaining wrap. Fold the edges under and crimp. Cover loosely with plastic wrap and refrigerate while you prepare the streusel topping and filling.

TO MAKE STREUSEL TOPPING:

Preheat oven to 375°F. In a bowl, stir together flour, sugar and lemon zest. Add butter, oil and lemon juice and work in with your fingertips until the mixture forms small crumbs; set aside.

TO MAKE FILLING AND BAKE PIE:

In a mixing bowl, stir together sugar and tapioca. Stir in lemon zest and juice. Add blueberries and stir gently to mix. Spoon the filling into the prepared crust. Cover loosely with foil and set in the middle of the oven, with a baking sheet placed on the rack below to catch any drips. Bake for 55 to 65 minutes, or until the berries are juicy and bubbling. (Frozen berries will take about 10 minutes longer.) Uncover the pie, sprinkle evenly with the reserved streusel topping and bake for 12 to 15 minutes longer, or until the streusel is golden. Cool on a wire rack for 30 minutes, then cool completely in the refrigerator, about 2 hours.

Serves 8.

315 calories per serving: 3 grams protein, 10 grams fat (2 grams saturated fat), 55 grams carbohydrate; 68 mg sodium; 8 mg cholesterol.

CRUST

- 1 cup all-purpose white flour
- 1 tablespoon sugar
- ⅛ teaspoon salt
- 1 tablespoon butter
- 3 tablespoons canola oil

STREUSEL TOPPING

- ¾ cup all-purpose white flour
- ¼ cup sugar
- 1 teaspoon grated lemon zest
- 1 tablespoon butter
- 1 tablespoon canola oil
- 1 tablespoon fresh lemon juice

FILLING

- ½ cup sugar
- 1½ tablespoons "minute" tapioca
- 1 teaspoon grated lemon zest
- 1 tablespoon fresh lemon juice
- 5 cups fresh *or* frozen unsweetened blueberries

KEY LIME PIE

The availability of nonfat sweetened condensed milk and nonfat yogurt have made it quite easy to transform a high-fat classic into a low-fat delight.

CRUST

1	large egg white
1½	cups graham cracker crumbs (12 whole crackers) (*see tip on page 140*)
1½	tablespoons butter, melted
1½	tablespoons canola oil

FILLING

1	14-ounce can nonfat sweetened condensed milk
⅔	cup nonfat plain yogurt
2	teaspoons grated lime zest
½	cup fresh lime juice, preferably from Key limes

TO MAKE CRUST:

1. Preheat oven to 350°F. Lightly oil a 9-inch pie pan or coat it with nonstick cooking spray.

2. In a mixing bowl, whisk egg white until frothy. Add graham cracker crumbs, butter and oil and blend with a fork or your fingertips until thoroughly combined. Press the mixture in an even layer on the bottom and sides of the pie pan.

3. Bake for 10 minutes, or until lightly browned. (Do not be concerned if there are small cracks.) Cool on a wire rack.

TO MAKE FILLING:

In a metal mixing bowl, whisk together sweetened condensed milk, yogurt, lime zest and juice. (The metal bowl will allow the filling to cool quickly over ice.) In a small bowl, sprinkle gelatin over 2 tablespoons cold water; let soften for 1 minute, then set the bowl in a skillet of simmering water and stir until the gelatin dissolves completely. Whisk the gelatin into the lime filling. Set the mixing bowl in a larger bowl of ice cubes, stirring occasionally, until it begins to thicken, 15 to 20 minutes. Spread in the pie shell, cover with plastic wrap and refrigerate until firm, about 1 hour.

TO MAKE MERINGUE:

1. Preheat broiler. Bring about 1 inch of water to a simmer in a large saucepan. Put sugar, egg whites, cream of tartar and 2 tablespoons of water in a metal bowl that will fit over the saucepan. Set the bowl over the simmering water and beat with an electric mixer on low speed, moving the beaters around the bowl constantly, until an instant-read thermometer registers 140°F. (This will take 3 to 5 minutes.)

2. Increase the mixer speed to high and continue beating over the heat for 3½ minutes. Remove the bowl from the heat and beat the meringue until cool, about 4 minutes. Beat in vanilla.

3. Top the chilled pie with the meringue, spreading it all the way to the edges and swirling it into peaks. Broil until the meringue is lightly browned, about 2 minutes. Chill the pie for 30 minutes before serving. Garnish with lime slices, if desired.

Serves 8.

295 calories per serving: 8 grams protein, 5 grams fat (2 grams saturated fat), 53 grams carbohydrate; 158 mg sodium; 13 mg cholesterol.

1   envelope plain gelatin
     (2 teaspoons)

MERINGUE

½   cup sugar

2   large egg whites

¼   teaspoon cream of tartar

1   teaspoon pure vanilla
     extract

     Thin slices fresh lime for
     garnish (optional)

◆**KEY LIMES VS. PERSIAN LIMES**

Key limes are rather small, yellow-to-green fruit with a very pungent flavor. The more familiar Persian limes are larger and darker green. For ½ cup juice, you will need 6 to 8 Key limes or 4 to 5 Persian limes.

Upside-Down Apple Pie

UPSIDE-DOWN APPLE PIE

Similar to the classic French Tarte Tatin—with the exception of the crust. Instead of high-fat puff pastry, the tart is baked under a layer of bread, which contributes almost no fat and bakes to a toasty golden brown.

TO PREPARE CARAMELIZED APPLES:

1. Preheat oven to 375°F. Lightly oil a 9-inch round cake pan or coat it with nonstick cooking spray. Melt butter in a heavy skillet over medium heat. Stir in sugar and cook over medium heat, without stirring, until the sugar caramelizes, 5 to 7 minutes. Add orange juice carefully; the mixture will sputter.

2. Peel, halve and core the apples; cut each half into 3 wedges. Add the apple wedges to the skillet, cover and cook until they release their juices, 4 to 5 minutes. Increase the heat to high, uncover and cook until the juices have been reduced to a thick glaze, 2 to 4 minutes. Remove from the heat. Push the apples to one side of the skillet. Spoon out as much caramel as possible from the skillet into the prepared cake pan. Set the apple wedges, rounded sides down, in a circular pattern in the caramel.

TO PREPARE CRUST AND BAKE TART:

1. Trim the crusts from the bread and cut each slice diagonally into 2 triangles. Arrange the triangles over the apples to form a single layer, cutting small pieces of bread as necessary to fill in the gaps. In a small bowl, stir together cider, oil and melted butter; brush lightly over the bread.

2. Bake for 25 minutes, or until the bread is crisp and golden brown. Cool the tart in the pan on a wire rack for about 10 minutes. Set a serving plate on top of the tart and quickly invert it. Reposition any apple pieces that stick to the pan, and drizzle any excess caramel over the top. Serve warm.

Serves 8.

180 calories per serving: 1 gram protein, 4 grams fat (1 gram saturated fat), 36 grams carbohydrate; 76 mg sodium; 4 mg cholesterol.

CARAMELIZED APPLES

- 2 teaspoons butter
- ⅔ cup sugar
- ½ cup fresh orange juice (1 orange)
- 1½ pounds cooking apples, such as Golden Delicious, Rome Beauty *or* Newtown Pippin (about 4)

BREAD CRUST

- 8 slices thin-sliced firm white bread (such as Pepperidge Farm)
- 2 tablespoons apple cider
- 1 tablespoon canola oil
- ½ tablespoon melted butter

GINGERY KUMQUAT & CRANBERRY TART

A rather wild and wonderful finish to a holiday meal. Kumquats, with their sweet, orange-flavored rind and tangy flesh, are a lively match for puckery cranberries.

FILLING

16	kumquats, thinly sliced and seeded, *or* 1 unpeeled orange, thinly sliced then chopped
2	cups fresh *or* frozen cranberries
½	cup sugar
⅓	cup currants
2	tablespoons chopped crystallized ginger (*see page 9*)

CRUST

1¾	cups all-purpose white flour
½	teaspoon baking powder
½	teaspoon baking soda
½	teaspoon salt
1	cup sugar
2	tablespoons butter, softened
2	tablespoons canola oil
1	large egg
2	teaspoons grated lemon zest
4-5	teaspoons fresh lemon juice
	Confectioners' sugar for dusting

♦**CHOOSING KUMQUATS**

A curious fruit in that the rind is often sweeter than the flesh. Look for firm, unblemished kumquats in the produce section in late fall and winter.

TO MAKE FILLING:

In a saucepan, combine kumquats or chopped orange, cranberries, sugar, currants and ginger with ⅔ cup water and bring to a simmer. Cook over low heat until the fruit is tender and the mixture is thick, 3 to 5 minutes. Set aside and let cool to room temperature.

TO MAKE CRUST AND BAKE TART:

1. Place rack in lower third of oven; preheat to 350°F. Lightly oil an 11-inch tart pan, preferably with a removable bottom, or coat it with nonstick cooking spray.

2. In a small bowl, stir together flour, baking powder, baking soda and salt. In a large bowl, beat together sugar, butter, oil, egg, lemon zest and 4 teaspoons lemon juice with an electric mixer until smooth. Beat in the dry ingredients until completely blended. (Dough should be moist. Add a bit more lemon juice if it does not press together easily.) Turn the dough out onto a work surface and knead four or five times.

3. Divide the dough in half. Working through a piece of plastic wrap so the dough doesn't stick to your hand, evenly press half of the dough into the bottom and up the sides of the tart pan. Spoon in the reserved kumquat-cranberry filling and spread evenly.

4. On a floured work surface, roll out the remaining dough into an 11-inch circle. Cut the circle into ½-inch-wide strips. Run a long spatula under the strips to loosen them. Lay half of the strips about ¾ inch apart on top of the filling. (Do not worry if the strips break—simply piece them end-to-end. If the strips are extremely fragile, gather them up, knead them briefly, then reroll.) Lay the remaining strips diagonally across the first strips. Press the ends of the strips into the edge of the crust, removing any excess.

5. Bake the tart for 30 to 40 minutes, or until the pastry is well-browned. Let the tart cool in the pan on a wire rack, covered with a clean towel to soften the top crust slightly. Dust the top lightly with confectioners' sugar.

Serves 10.

290 calories per serving: 3 grams protein, 6 grams fat (2 grams saturated fat), 58 grams carbohydrate; 198 mg sodium; 27 mg cholesterol.

NEW ENGLAND APPLE PIE

Apple butter adds to the mellow fruitiness of this harvest pie.

TO MAKE CRUST:

1. In a medium bowl, stir together flour, sugar and salt. In a small saucepan, melt butter over low heat. Cook, swirling the pan, until the butter turns a nutty brown, about 30 seconds. Pour into a small bowl and let cool. Stir in oil. Using a fork, slowly stir the butter-oil mixture into the flour until the mixture is crumbly. Gradually stir in enough ice water (1 to 2 tablespoons) so that the dough will hold together. Press the dough into a flattened disk.

2. Place two overlapping lengths of plastic wrap on the work surface. Set the dough in the center and cover with two more sheets of plastic wrap. With a rolling pin, roll the dough into a circle about 12 inches in diameter. Remove the top sheets and invert the dough into a 9-inch pie pan. Gently press the dough into the bottom of the pie pan. Remove the remaining wrap. Fold the edges under and crimp. Cover loosely with plastic wrap and refrigerate while you prepare the filling and topping.

TO MAKE FILLING AND TOPPING:

1. Preheat oven to 375°F. Place currants and cranberries in a steamer over simmering water; cover the pan and steam the fruit for 5 minutes, or until softened. Transfer to a mixing bowl and stir in apples, apple butter and cinnamon until well mixed. Spoon the filling into the prepared pie crust. Cover the pie loosely with foil and set in the middle of the oven, with a baking sheet placed on the rack below to catch any drips. Bake for 50 to 60 minutes, or until the filling is bubbling on the edges and the apples are tender.

2. Meanwhile, in a small bowl, work together oats, flour and brown sugar with a fork or your fingertips until there are no large lumps of brown sugar. Drizzle oil and ½ tablespoon water over the top and work together until the mixture forms small crumbs.

3. Uncover the pie and distribute the topping evenly over the apples. Bake, uncovered, for 10 to 15 minutes longer, or until the topping is golden. Serve warm or cooled.

Serves 8.

355 calories per serving: 4 grams protein, 10 grams fat (2 grams saturated fat), 65 grams carbohydrate; 52 mg sodium; 4 mg cholesterol.

CRUST

- 1 cup all-purpose white flour
- 1 tablespoon sugar
- ⅛ teaspoon salt
- 1 tablespoon butter
- 3 tablespoons canola oil

FILLING

- ½ cup currants
- ½ cup dried cranberries
- 6 cups thinly sliced peeled cooking apples, such as Cortland, Granny Smith *or* Golden Delicious (about 6 large apples)
- ⅔ cup apple butter
- ½ teaspoon ground cinnamon

TOPPING

- ⅓ cup "quick" *or* regular rolled oats
- ⅓ cup all-purpose white flour
- ⅓ cup packed light brown sugar
- 1½ tablespoons canola oil

MINCEMEAT TART

The filling for this Thanksgiving standard is rich, dark and spicy, yet it has a fresher flavor than mincemeat from a jar.

FILLING

- 2 juicy apples, such as McIntosh, peeled, cored and diced
- 2 ripe pears, peeled, cored and diced
- ½ unpeeled navel orange, scrubbed and chopped
- ½ cup raisins
- ½ cup chopped dried figs
- ½ cup chopped dried tart cherries
- ½ cup packed dark brown sugar
- 2 tablespoons fresh lemon juice
- ½ teaspoon ground cinnamon
- ¼ teaspoon ground allspice
- ⅛ teaspoon ground cloves
  Pinch of salt
- 3 tablespoons brandy *or* fresh orange juice
- 1 tablespoon butter

DOUGH

- 1¼ cups all-purpose white flour
- 1 tablespoon plus 1 teaspoon sugar
- 1 teaspoon active dry yeast
- 1 tablespoon canola oil
- ¼ teaspoon salt
- 1 egg, lightly beaten with 2 teaspoons water, for glazing

TO MAKE FILLING:

In a large saucepan, combine apples, pears, chopped orange, raisins, figs, cherries, brown sugar, lemon juice, cinnamon, allspice, cloves and salt. Pour in 1½ cups water, bring to a simmer, cover the pan and cook over low heat, stirring occasionally, for 60 to 70 minutes, or until the fruits are very tender. Uncover the pan and continue cooking until the mincemeat is very thick and the juices have evaporated, about 10 minutes longer. Stir in brandy or orange juice and butter and let cool to room temperature.

TO MAKE DOUGH:

Meanwhile, in a mixing bowl, stir together ½ cup of the flour, 1 tablespoon of the sugar, yeast and ½ cup warm water; let stand until the yeast starts to bubble, about 5 minutes. Stir in oil and salt. Stir in the remaining flour, ¼ cup at a time, until the dough becomes too difficult to stir. Turn the dough out onto a lightly floured work surface and knead, adding additional flour if necessary, until the dough is firm and satiny but not dry, about 5 minutes. (Be careful not to add too much flour.) Place the dough in an oiled bowl, cover with plastic wrap, and let rise until doubled in bulk, about 45 minutes to 1 hour.

TO ASSEMBLE AND BAKE TART:

1. Place rack in lower third of oven and preheat to 375°F. Lightly oil an 11-inch tart pan, preferably with a removable bottom, or coat it with nonstick cooking spray.

2. Set one-fourth of the dough aside. On a lightly floured surface, roll out the remaining dough into a 15-inch circle. Fit the dough into the prepared tart pan, letting the dough hang over the edges of the pan. Spread the mincemeat filling in the pan. Fold the edges of the dough in over the filling.

3. Roll out the reserved dough on the floured surface. With a paring knife, cut out leaf shapes and set

them on top of the mincemeat. Lightly brush the leaves and border of the dough with egg glaze and sprinkle with the remaining 1 teaspoon sugar. Bake for 30 to 40 minutes, or until the crust is golden on top and browned on the bottom. If the top of the tart is browning too quickly, cover it loosely with aluminum foil.

4. Place the tart on a wire rack to cool slightly. Remove the rim of the pan and serve the tart warm or at room temperature.

Serves 12.

195 calories per serving: 2 grams protein, 3 grams fat (1 gram saturated fat), 42 grams carbohydrate; 59 mg sodium; 3 mg cholesterol.

◆**NUTRITION NOTE**
Our tart is low in fat and high in vitamins and minerals from the rich complement of fruits.

Mincemeat Tart

PROVENÇAL PEAR TART

A rustic confection that is traditional on Christmas Eve in Provence. The tart is best when served within two hours of baking.

FILLING

1½   pounds ripe pears, such as Bosc *or* Anjou, peeled, cored and coarsely chopped (4-5 pears)

1   tablespoon brown sugar

¼   teaspoon aniseed

DOUGH

1¼   cups all-purpose white flour

2   teaspoons sugar

1   teaspoon active dry yeast

1   tablespoon canola oil

½   teaspoon salt

1   egg, lightly beaten with 2 teaspoons water, for glazing

TO MAKE FILLING:

In a heavy saucepan, combine pears and brown sugar. Add ¼ cup water and bring to a boil over medium-high heat. Reduce the heat to low and cook, covered, stirring occasionally, for 30 minutes. Mash to a chunky puree with a potato masher. Continue to simmer, uncovered, stirring often, until very thick, about 20 minutes. Stir in aniseed and cool to room temperature. (*The filling can be made up to 2 days in advance and stored, covered, in the refrigerator. Bring to room temperature before proceeding.*)

TO MAKE DOUGH:

Meanwhile, in a mixing bowl, stir together ½ cup of the flour, sugar, yeast and ½ cup warm water; let stand 5 minutes. Stir in oil and salt. Stir in the remaining flour, ¼ cup at a time, until the dough becomes too difficult to stir. Turn the dough out onto a lightly floured work surface and knead, adding additional flour if necessary, until the dough is firm and satiny but not dry, about 5 minutes. Place the dough in an oiled bowl, cover with plastic wrap, and let rise until doubled in bulk, about 45 minutes to 1 hour.

TO ASSEMBLE AND BAKE TART:

1. Position rack in lower third of oven and preheat to 375°F. Lightly oil an 11-inch tart pan, preferably with a removable bottom, or coat it with nonstick cooking spray.

2. Set one-third of the dough aside. On a lightly floured surface, roll out the remaining dough into a 14-inch circle. Fit the dough into the prepared tart pan, letting the dough hang slightly over the edges of the pan. Roll out the remaining dough into a 10½-inch circle and cut it into 16 strips ¼ inch wide.

3. Spread the filling in the pan. Lay 8 of the strips across the filling, pressing the ends into the edge. Lay the remaining strips on top at an angle to create a crisscross pattern. Fold the edge of the dough over the ends. Lightly brush the dough with egg glaze.

4. Bake for 30 to 40 minutes, or until the crust is golden. If the tart browns too quickly, cover loosely with foil. Cool on a wire rack.

Serves 8.

150 calories per serving: 3 grams protein, 2 grams fat (0 grams saturated fat), 31 grams carbohydrate; 134 mg sodium; 0 mg cholesterol.

LEMON CREAM PIE

A refreshing finish to a meal at any time of the year.

TO MAKE CRUST:

Preheat oven to 350°F. Lightly oil a 9-inch pie pan or coat it with nonstick cooking spray. In a medium bowl, whisk egg white until frothy. Add graham cracker crumbs, butter and oil and blend with a fork or your fingertips until thoroughly combined. Press the mixture in an even layer on the bottom and sides of the pie pan. Bake for 10 minutes, or until lightly browned. (Do not be concerned if there are small cracks.) Cool on a wire rack.

TO MAKE FILLING:

1. Line a colander or strainer with cheesecloth or coffee filters and set over a bowl. Spoon in yogurt and let drain in the refrigerator until it measures 1½ cups, 45 minutes to 1 hour.

2. Meanwhile, in a heavy nonreactive saucepan, stir together sugar and lemon juice. Bring to a boil and cook over medium-low heat until the syrup reaches 239°F on a candy thermometer (soft-ball stage), about 3 minutes. To be sure the syrup has reached the proper temperature, spoon a few drops into a glass of ice water; it should form a soft ball on the bottom of the glass. Remove the syrup from the heat and pour it into a mixing bowl.

3. In a small bowl, sprinkle gelatin over ⅓ cup cold water. Let soften for 5 minutes, then whisk into the lemon syrup until completely dissolved. Set the syrup aside to cool for 1 hour. (*Alternatively, set the bowl of syrup into a larger bowl of ice and stir occasionally until cool.*)

4. Whisk the drained yogurt and lemon zest into the cooled syrup. Refrigerate until very cool, stirring occasionally, about 1 hour. (*Or, again, stir over ice.*) To enhance the color, add about 2 drops of yellow food coloring, if desired.

5. In a chilled bowl, whip cream until moderately stiff; fold into the yogurt mixture. Spoon the filling into the crust and refrigerate until firm, about 2 hours. Just before serving, garnish with lemon slices and mint sprigs. (*The pie can be made up to 1 day ahead.*)

Serves 8.

280 calories per serving: 6 grams protein, 10 grams fat (5 grams saturated fat), 44 grams carbohydrate; 128 mg sodium; 23 mg cholesterol.

CRUST

- 1 large egg white
- 1½ cups graham cracker crumbs (12 whole crackers) (*see tip on page 140*)
- 1½ tablespoons butter, melted
- 1½ tablespoons canola oil

FILLING

- 2 cups nonfat vanilla yogurt
- 1¼ cups sugar
- ½ cup fresh lemon juice
- 1 envelope plain gelatin (2 teaspoons)
- 1 teaspoon grated lemon zest
  Yellow food coloring (optional)
- ½ cup whipping cream
  Lemon slices and mint leaves for garnish

◆**DRAINING YOGURT**
Avoid yogurts with added starch, gums or gelatin, as these will not drain and thicken properly.

Banana-Chocolate Dream Pie

BANANA-CHOCOLATE DREAM PIE

Creamy, dark and delectable, this is a grownup version of a childhood pleasure.

CRUST

1	cup all-purpose white flour
1	tablespoon sugar
⅛	teaspoon salt
1	tablespoon butter
3	tablespoons canola oil

TO MAKE CRUST:

1. Coat a 9-inch pie pan with nonstick cooking spray. In a medium bowl, stir together flour, sugar and salt. In a small saucepan, melt butter over low heat. Cook, swirling the pan, until the butter turns a nutty brown, about 30 seconds. Pour into a small bowl and stir in oil. Using a fork, slowly stir the butter-oil mixture into the flour until the mixture is crumbly. Gradually stir in enough ice water (1 to 2 tablespoons) so that the dough will hold together. Press the dough into a flattened disk.

2. Place two overlapping lengths of plastic wrap on the work surface. Set the dough in the center and cover with two more sheets of plastic wrap. With a rolling pin, roll the dough into a circle about 12 inches in diameter. Remove the top sheets and invert the dough over the prepared pie pan. Gently press the dough into the bottom of the pie pan. Remove the remaining wrap. Fold the edges under and crimp. Prick the bottom with a fork. Cover and place in the freezer for 10 minutes. Meanwhile, preheat oven to 400°F.

3. Line the pastry shell with a piece of foil or parchment paper and fill with pie weights or dried beans. Bake for 10 minutes. Remove paper and weights. Protect the edges with strips of aluminum foil. Bake for 10 to 12 minutes longer, or until the crust is golden. Cool on a wire rack. Reduce oven temperature to 350°F.

TO MAKE FILLING:

1. In a mixing bowl, whisk together ¼ cup of the evaporated skim milk, egg, brown sugar, cocoa and cornstarch. In a heavy saucepan, heat the remaining 1 cup evaporated skim milk over medium heat until steaming. Whisk the hot milk into the egg mixture. Return the mixture to the pan and cook over medium heat, whisking constantly, until the mixture bubbles and thickens, about 2 minutes. Remove from the heat and add chocolate, stirring until it has melted. Stir in coffee liqueur and vanilla.

2. Peel and thinly slice bananas, arranging in the bottom of the baked pie shell. Spoon in the chocolate filling, spreading evenly. Set aside while you make the meringue.

TO MAKE MERINGUE:

In a large bowl, beat egg whites with an electric mixer until frothy. Add cream of tartar and beat until soft peaks form. Slowly add sugar, beating until the mixture holds stiff, shiny peaks. Blend in vanilla. Spread the meringue over the filling, sealing to the edge of the crust. With a metal spatula or the back of a spoon, make attractive peaks. Bake for 15 minutes at 350°F; the top should be beautifully browned. Cool the pie on a wire rack for about 2 hours before serving.

Serves 8.

305 calories per serving: 7 grams protein, 9 grams fat (2 grams saturated fat), 50 grams carbohydrate; 126 mg sodium; 32 mg cholesterol.

FILLING

1¼ cups evaporated skim milk

1 large egg

⅓ cup packed light brown sugar

3 tablespoons unsweetened cocoa powder, preferably Dutch-process

1 tablespoon cornstarch

1 ounce bittersweet (*not* unsweetened) chocolate, coarsely chopped

1 tablespoon Kahlúa *or* other coffee-flavored liqueur

1 teaspoon pure vanilla extract

2 large *or* 3 small ripe, but firm, bananas

MERINGUE

3 large egg whites

¼ teaspoon cream of tartar

½ cup granulated sugar

1 teaspoon pure vanilla extract

◆**INGREDIENT NOTE**

Cream of tartar improves stability and volume in beaten egg whites.

PUMPKIN PIE WITH RUM

Dark molasses and dark rum put this pumpkin pie a cut above all the rest. If you do not have a 9-inch deep-dish pie pan, use a standard 9-inch pie pan and bake the extra filling in a custard cup.

CRUST

¾ cup all-purpose white flour

¼ cup whole-wheat flour

1 tablespoon sugar

⅛ teaspoon salt

1 tablespoon butter

3 tablespoons canola oil

FILLING

2 large eggs, lightly beaten

1 15- *or* 16-ounce can plain pumpkin puree (1½ cups)

1 12-ounce can evaporated skim milk

¼ cup dark molasses

3 tablespoons dark rum *or* 1 tablespoon vanilla

½ cup packed dark brown sugar

1 tablespoon cornstarch

1 teaspoon ground cinnamon

1 teaspoon ground ginger

¼ teaspoon freshly grated nutmeg

¼ teaspoon salt

TO MAKE CRUST:

1. In a medium bowl, stir together white and whole-wheat flours, sugar and salt. In a small saucepan, melt butter over low heat. Cook, swirling the pan, until the butter turns a nutty brown, about 30 seconds. Pour into a small bowl and let cool. Stir in oil. Using a fork, slowly stir the butter-oil mixture into the flour until the mixture is crumbly. Gradually stir in enough ice water (1 to 2 tablespoons) so that the dough will hold together. Press the dough into a flattened disk.

2. Place two overlapping lengths of plastic wrap on the work surface. Set the dough in the center and cover with two more sheets of plastic wrap. With a rolling pin, roll the dough into a circle about 13 inches in diameter. Remove the top sheets and invert the dough into a 9-inch deep-dish pie pan. Remove the remaining wrap. Fold the edges under at the rim and crimp. Cover loosely with plastic wrap and refrigerate while you prepare the filling.

TO MAKE FILLING:

1. Position rack in lower third of oven; preheat to 350°F. In a mixing bowl, lightly whisk eggs. Add pumpkin, evaporated milk, molasses and rum or vanilla. In a small bowl, combine brown sugar, cornstarch, cinnamon, ginger, nutmeg and salt. Rub through a sieve into the pumpkin mixture and whisk until incorporated.

2. Pour the filling into the prepared crust and bake for 40 to 50 minutes, or until the filling has set and a skewer inserted in the center comes out clean. During baking, cover the edges with foil if they are browning too quickly. Cool on a wire rack.

Serves 8.

270 calories per serving: 7 grams protein, 8 grams fat (2 grams saturated fat), 44 grams carbohydrate; 188 mg sodium; 59 mg cholesterol.

◆**CHECK THE LABEL**
Don't use pumpkin-pie mix—buy canned pumpkin without added spices.

FRUITY FLOURISHES

The USDA Food Guide Pyramid counsels Americans to eat two to four servings of fruit every day. An excellent idea, but how many days go by when you haven't even had an apple? Simple fruit desserts are a deliciously effective way of getting the fruit you need.

It takes but a few moments to hull some strawberries or to cut up a melon; add a squeeze of

lemon and a whisper of sugar, and you have a universally pleasing finish to a meal. Throughout this chapter, subtle embellishments—a spoonful of honey or a well-chosen spice or a splash of liqueur—are used to bring out fruit's inherent goodness.

MIXED-BERRY CHAMPAGNE AMBROSIA

Any combination of berries or cherries (or nectarines or peaches, for that matter) can be used. Several colors make the prettiest presentation, but single-berry ambrosia is delicious too.

¼ cup honey, preferably berry-blossom honey

2 tablespoons fresh lime juice (1 lime)

2 large sprigs fresh mint plus 6 smaller sprigs for garnish

5 cups mixed fresh berries, such as raspberries, blueberries, tiny strawberries, blackberries *or* pitted Bing cherries

2 cups chilled Champagne *or* other sparkling white wine

1. In a small saucepan, combine honey, lime juice and large mint sprigs; warm over low heat just until the honey melts. Remove from the heat and let steep for 5 minutes; discard the mint. Place the fruit in a large bowl, pour the honey mixture over and stir gently to combine. Divide the berry mixture among 6 individual goblets or dessert dishes and refrigerate until ready to serve, up to 1 hour.

2. Just before serving, pour Champagne over the fruit. Garnish each serving with a sprig of mint and serve.

Serves 6.

145 calories per serving: 1 gram protein, 0 grams fat, 23 grams carbohydrate, 7 grams alcohol; 4 mg sodium; 0 mg cholesterol.

◆**FRESH BERRY ADVICE**

Summer berries are fragile, susceptible to mold and have a short storage life.

If possible, buy fruit at fruit stands, where minimal handling means fruit is in its prime.

Look for perfect, unblemished berries in dry, unstained containers.

Wash fresh berries just before using them to prevent moisture absorption.

Mixed-Berry Champagne Ambrosia

PEAR FRANGIPANE

Whole eggs, butter and almonds are essential ingredients in a high-fat frangipane. This low-fat interpretation maintains the richness of the almonds and cuts back on the fat by omitting the yolks and using only a bit of butter for flavor.

3   **firm but ripe pears, such as Bosc, Comice *or* Anjou**

2   **teaspoons fresh lemon juice**

2   **teaspoons butter, melted**

¼   **cup whole-wheat pastry flour (*see page 8*)**

¼   **teaspoon baking powder**

2   **large egg whites**

⅓   **cup frozen apple-juice concentrate, thawed**

¼   **teaspoon pure vanilla extract**

⅓   **cup ground almonds**

¼   **cup skim milk**

1. Preheat oven to 350°F. Lightly oil a 10-inch pie pan or quiche pan or coat it with nonstick cooking spray. Peel, halve and core pears. Set the pear halves flat-side-down on a cutting board. Cut crosswise into ½-inch-thick slices: keep the pear halves intact, not separating the slices. Brush the surface with lemon juice, then with melted butter.

2. In a small bowl, stir together flour and baking powder. In a mixing bowl, beat egg whites with an electric mixer until soft peaks form. Gradually add apple-juice concentrate and vanilla, beating until stiff peaks form. Fold in the dry ingredients and almonds. Gently stir in milk. (The batter will decrease in volume.) Turn the batter into the prepared pan.

3. To assemble the dessert, slide a metal spatula under a sliced pear half, pressing gently to fan it slightly, and set it stem-end-to-the-center on the batter. Repeat with remaining pear halves. Bake for 25 to 35 minutes, or until golden. Serve warm.

Serves 6.

150 calories per serving: 4 grams protein, 5 grams fat (1 gram saturated fat), 23 grams carbohydrate; 56 mg sodium; 4 mg cholesterol.

♦**GRINDING ALMONDS**

If you have whole, not ground, almonds, grind them in the food processor with a teaspoon of sugar. Do not overwork them or they will get oily.

SLICED ORANGES WITH WARM RASPBERRIES

Warming the berries enhances their flavor and makes a pleasing contrast to the cool orange slices. Fresh pineapple can stand in for the oranges.

1. With a sharp knife, remove and discard the skin and white pith from oranges; slice the oranges crosswise and arrange on 4 dessert plates.

2. In a small saucepan, combine sugar, lemon juice and cinnamon; stir over low heat until bubbling. Add raspberries and stir gently until the berries are warmed through or just thawed. Spoon over the orange slices and serve immediately.

Serves 4.

115 calories per serving: 2 grams protein, 1 gram fat (0 grams saturated fat), 29 grams carbohydrate; 0 mg sodium; 0 mg cholesterol.

4	seedless oranges, such as navel oranges
2	tablespoons sugar
1	tablespoon fresh lemon juice
¼	teaspoon ground cinnamon
2	cups fresh *or* frozen unsweetened raspberries (*not* thawed)

ROASTED PINEAPPLE

The natural sweetness of pineapple comes through particularly well when the fruit is roasted. Pepper adds an unexpected lively accent.

Preheat oven to 500°F. Slice off the top and bottom of pineapple and cut it into 8 slices, each about 1 inch thick. Rub the slices lightly with oil, sprinkle with pepper and place in a single layer on a baking sheet. Roast for 15 minutes, flip slices over and roast for an additional 10 minutes. The pineapple should be lightly browned on both sides. Remove from the oven and immediately sprinkle with brown sugar. (*The pineapple can be roasted up to 2 hours ahead of time; let it cool and then cover loosely with plastic wrap and leave at room temperature.*) Cut into wedges and serve with lime quarters for squeezing.

Serves 6.

80 calories per serving: 1 gram protein, 2 grams fat (0 grams saturated fat), 26 grams carbohydrate; 2 mg sodium; 0 mg cholesterol.

1	large ripe pineapple
2	teaspoons canola oil
	Freshly ground black pepper to taste
2	tablespoons brown sugar
2	limes, quartered

◆**FRESH PINEAPPLE**

A perfectly ripe pineapple will have a fruity aroma and a slight "give" when pressed. Keep it in the refrigerator to prevent further ripening.

Brandied Nectarines

BRANDIED NECTARINES

Perfumed with vanilla and brandy, these nectarines are elegant in their simplicity. Use only perfectly ripe, juicy fruit.

½ cup brandy, preferably Cognac

2 tablespoons sugar

1-inch piece of vanilla bean

4 medium nectarines, halved and pitted

1. In a skillet large enough to hold the nectarines in a single layer, stir together brandy and sugar. Add vanilla bean. Place nectarines cut-side down in the skillet and bring to a simmer over low heat. (Be careful working over a gas burner, as the warm brandy is quite flammable.) Cover the pan and simmer the nectarines for 10 to 15 minutes, or until just tender when pierced with a skewer. Check occasionally to be sure the nectarines are not sticking to the bottom of the skillet.

2. Remove the pan from the heat, uncover and let cool briefly; slip off and discard the nectarine skins if they come away easily. Transfer the nectarines cut-side up to a serving dish and spoon the syrup over the top. Serve warm.

Serves 4.

90 calories per serving: 1 gram protein, 0 grams fat, 22 grams carbohydrate; 0 mg sodium; 0 mg cholesterol.

SCALLOPED BANANAS

Eating Well Test Kitchen Director Patsy Jamieson developed this recipe for an April Fool's Day feature. The banana pieces resemble fried scallops and the Vanilla Cream looks like tartar sauce.

1. Preheat oven to 450°F. Line a baking sheet with aluminum foil. Set a rack on top and coat it with nonstick cooking spray.

2. In a shallow dish, combine gingersnap crumbs, oil and butter. Mix with your fingertips until well blended; set aside. In a medium bowl, whisk together egg white, brown sugar and lemon juice; set aside.

3. Peel bananas and trim pointed tips. Cut bananas crosswise into ¾-inch pieces. Dip about 6 pieces into the egg-white mixture, then, with 2 forks, transfer them to the crumb mixture. With 2 clean forks, roll the banana pieces in the crumbs until evenly coated. Place on the prepared rack. Repeat with the remaining banana pieces.

4. Bake until crisp, golden and heated through, about 8 to 12 minutes. Arrange the hot bananas on dessert plates, garnish with lemon wedges and mint sprigs and pass the Vanilla Cream separately, if using.

Serves 4.

255 calories per serving: 3 grams protein, 6 grams fat (1 gram saturated fat), 49 grams carbohydrate; 236 mg sodium; 3 mg cholesterol.

1 cup gingersnap crumbs (about 16 cookies)

2 teaspoons canola oil

1 teaspoon butter, melted

1 large egg white

2 tablespoons dark brown sugar

1 teaspoon fresh lemon juice

3 large ripe, but firm bananas

Lemon wedges and mint sprigs for garnish

½ cup Vanilla Cream (*page 182*), optional

♦**INGREDIENT NOTE**

For this recipe and others in this book, use commercial "old-fashioned" gingersnaps—the small, flat ones sold in a box. They are quite flavorful and very low in fat. Turn cookies into crumbs in a food processor, or place them between two sheets of wax paper and roll them with a rolling pin.

MELON BALLS IN PORT

A traditional pairing updated with a little lime juice.

⅓ cup tawny port
1 tablespoon honey
1 tablespoon fresh lime juice
½ teaspoon grated lime zest
5 crushed mint leaves
1½ cups cantaloupe balls
1½ cups honeydew melon balls
Fresh mint for garnish

In a bowl, stir together port, honey, lime juice, lime zest and mint leaves until the honey is dissolved. Add cantaloupe and honeydew melon balls and stir gently to coat them. Cover with plastic wrap and chill in the refrigerator for 30 minutes, stirring every 10 minutes or so. Serve garnished with fresh mint leaves.

Serves 4.

95 calories per serving: 1 gram protein, 0 grams fat, 17 grams carbohydrate, 5 grams alcohol; 13 mg sodium; 0 mg cholesterol.

CHERRY AMARETTI GRATIN

Sweet amaretti crumbs make a quick, low-fat topping that is a perfect foil for tart cherries.

4 cups tart cherries
   (about 1½ pounds), pitted
1 tablespoon fresh lemon
   juice
1 tablespoon Amaretto *or*
   other almond liqueur
   (optional)
1 tablespoon cornstarch
1 cup coarsely crushed
   amaretti crumbs
   (about 18 amaretti)
1 tablespoon brown sugar
   Confectioners' sugar for
   dusting

1. Preheat oven to 400°F. In a bowl, toss cherries with lemon juice, Amaretto, if using, and cornstarch. Spoon the fruit into a 1-quart gratin dish or pie pan or into 4 individual ovenproof dishes.

2. In a small bowl, stir together amaretti crumbs and brown sugar. Sprinkle evenly over the cherry mixture. Bake for 20 to 30 minutes, or until the cherries are bubbling and the topping is golden. Let cool for 15 minutes. Dust with confectioners' sugar and serve.

Serves 4.

170 calories per serving: 2 grams protein, 1 gram fat (0 grams saturated fat), 41 grams carbohydrate; 153 mg sodium; 0 mg cholesterol.

◆**SPECIAL EQUIPMENT**
Invest in a cherry pitter.
This handy tool makes the pitting go much more quickly.

TROPICAL FRUIT COMPOTE

Whole spices will infuse poaching liquids with subtle but distinct flavors. Here fruit is not cooked in the syrup, but simply macerated so that the tastes remain fresh and distinct. The spiced syrup is also a wonderful sweetener for hot tea or a base for a light punch.

1. In a small saucepan, combine sugar, pineapple juice, lime juice and zest. Tie the cardamom pods, allspice berries, peppercorns, cloves and cinnamon sticks in a square of cheesecloth and add to the saucepan. Bring the liquid to a boil, stirring to dissolve the sugar. Cover the pan, reduce the heat to low and simmer gently for 10 minutes. Remove from the heat and let cool. Stir in orange liqueur or vanilla. Cover and refrigerate for at least 30 minutes or up to 24 hours.

2. Toss the fruit in a serving bowl. Add the syrup and stir gently. Refrigerate for 30 minutes. Remove the spices and serve.

Makes about 4 cups, serves 6.

210 calories per serving: 2 grams protein, 1 gram fat (0 grams saturated fat), 52 grams carbohydrate, 2 grams alcohol; 6 mg sodium; 0 mg cholesterol.

½	cup sugar
½	cup unsweetened pineapple juice
¼	cup fresh lime juice (2 limes)
1	teaspoon grated lime zest
10	whole cardamom pods, lightly crushed
8	whole allspice berries
8	whole black peppercorns
8	whole cloves
2	cinnamon sticks, broken in half
2	tablespoons Curaçao *or* other orange liqueur *or* 1 teaspoon pure vanilla extract
3	kiwi fruit, peeled and sliced
2	mangoes *or* papayas, peeled, seeded and cut into chunks
2	seedless tangerines *or* small oranges, peeled and sliced
2	carambolas (star fruit), thinly sliced
1	cup fresh pineapple chunks
1	banana, sliced

◆**PEELING MANGOES**

The easy way to cut up a mango is to stand it up and slice the skin and fruit from each side as a single piece, just clearing the long, flat seed. Score the flesh in small cubes through to the skin, press the skin so the cut side pops out like a hand grenade, and slice the cubes off the skin.

BAKED FIGS WITH RASPBERRIES & YOGURT CREAM

Figs warm from the oven, cool yogurt cream and juicy fresh raspberries make a sublime trio.

1 cup nonfat plain yogurt

⅓ cup light whipping cream

3 tablespoons confectioners' sugar

1 teaspoon eau-de-vie de framboise *or* kirsch (optional)

8 ripe fresh figs, quartered lengthwise

1 tablespoon granulated sugar

1 tablespoon fresh lemon juice

1 cup fresh raspberries

1. Line a small strainer with cheesecloth or a paper coffee filter and set it over a bowl. Spoon in yogurt and let it drain in the refrigerator until reduced to ½ cup, about 2 hours.

2. In a chilled mixing bowl, beat cream to soft peaks. Add the drained yogurt, confectioners' sugar and framboise or kirsch; fold in with a rubber spatula. (*The yogurt cream may be used immediately or refrigerated, covered, for up to 8 hours.*)

3. Preheat oven to 450°F. In a shallow ovenproof baking dish, arrange figs in a single layer, cut-side up. Sprinkle with granulated sugar and lemon juice. Bake for 15 minutes, or until the figs are heated through and the sugar has melted.

4. Spoon the yogurt cream into 4 dessert dishes. Set the warm figs on top and garnish with raspberries. Serve immediately.

Serves 4.

210 calories per serving: 5 grams protein, 7 grams fat (4 grams saturated fat), 36 grams carbohydrate; 51 mg sodium; 23 mg cholesterol.

◆**SELECTING FRESH FIGS**

Fresh figs have fragile skin and bruise easily; choose blemish-free fruit.
When ripe they are slightly soft and have a mild, sweet scent.
There are green and purple varieties; either will work in this recipe.

Baked Figs with Raspberries & Yogurt Cream

STONE-FRUIT SOUP

A colorful and unusual finale to dinner, and great for breakfast as well.

½ cup dried apricots, thinly sliced

½ cup dried peaches, diced

2 tablespoons sugar

2 cinnamon sticks

1 vanilla bean, split lengthwise

1½ teaspoons cornstarch

½ cup dried tart cherries

2 tablespoons fresh lemon juice

1. In a saucepan, combine apricots, peaches, sugar, cinnamon sticks, vanilla bean and 6 cups water. Bring to a boil, reduce the heat and simmer until the fruit is tender, about 15 minutes.

2. In a small dish, stir together cornstarch and 2 tablespoons cold water. Add the cornstarch mixture to the simmering soup, stirring constantly, until the soup thickens slightly. Remove from the heat and stir in cherries and lemon juice. Cover the pan and let the cherries plump for about 15 minutes. Remove the cinnamon sticks and vanilla bean before serving.

Makes about 6 cups, serves 6.

105 calories per serving: 1 gram protein, 0 grams fat, 27 grams carbohydrate; 3 mg sodium; 0 mg cholesterol.

APPLES POACHED IN WHITE WINE

If you haven't cooked with a real vanilla bean, this simple dessert is a lovely way to experience its exquisite flavor.

2 cups dry white wine

½ cup sugar

4 Golden Delicious apples, peeled, quartered and cored

1 3-inch-long piece vanilla bean

1 3-inch-long strip lemon zest

1. In a large saucepan, heat wine and sugar over medium heat, stirring until the sugar dissolves. Add apples, vanilla bean and lemon zest and bring to a simmer. Reduce the heat to low, cover and cook until the apples are just tender when pierced with a skewer, 8 to 10 minutes. With a slotted spoon, transfer the apples to a serving bowl.

2. Rapidly boil the remaining poaching liquid over high heat until it is reduced to a syrup, about 15 minutes; spoon over the apples and refrigerate until chilled.

Serves 4.

250 calories per serving: 0 grams protein, 0 grams fat, 46 grams carbohydrate; 7 mg sodium; 0 mg cholesterol.

SPICED WINE & FRUIT

This recipe suggests a combination of plums and raspberries, but the spiced-wine syrup can be used with any seasonal fruits.

1. In a saucepan, combine wine, sugar and ¼ cup water. Bring to a boil. Tie vanilla bean, ginger and cinnamon stick in cheesecloth and add to the wine mixture. Reduce the heat to low and simmer for 3 minutes.

2. Add plums, cover and simmer gently for 5 to 7 minutes, turning once or twice, or until tender. Remove the pan from the heat and gently stir in raspberries and lemon juice. Let stand for 20 minutes. Discard the spices. (*The fruit can be prepared ahead and stored, covered, in the refrigerator for up to 2 days.*) Serve warm or cool, with yogurt, if desired.

Serves 4.

180 calories per serving: 0 grams protein, 0 grams fat, 49 grams carbohydrate; 3 mg sodium; 0 mg cholesterol.

1	cup white wine, preferably a slightly sweet Rhine *or* Mosel
½	cup sugar
½	vanilla bean, split lengthwise
4	thin slices peeled fresh ginger
½	cinnamon stick
1	pound prune plums (12-16), halved and pitted
1	cup fresh raspberries
1	tablespoon fresh lemon juice
1	cup nonfat vanilla yogurt (optional)

DRIED FRUIT COMPOTE

An easy winter dessert; leftovers are good at breakfast.

In a large saucepan, combine fruits, sugar, clove and cinnamon stick with 6 cups water. Bring to a simmer over medium heat. Cover the pan, reduce the heat to low and simmer until tender, 30 to 45 minutes. Remove the lemons, clove and cinnamon stick before serving warm or chilled.

Makes about 8 cups, serves 16.

120 calories per serving: 1 gram protein, 0 grams fat, 32 grams carbohydrate; 3 mg sodium; 0 mg cholesterol.

¾	pound pitted prunes
½	pound dried peaches, apples *or* pears
½	cup raisins
1	lemon, quartered
½	cup sugar
1	whole clove
1	cinnamon stick

CRANBERRY BAKED APPLES

Serve these pretty stuffed apples on their own or sitting in a pool of Vanilla Custard Sauce (page 182).

4 large cooking apples, such as Golden Delicious, Cortland *or* Rome

½ cup dried cranberries *or* currants

¼ cup packed light brown sugar

2 teaspoons butter

¼ cup apple cider *or* apple juice

1. Preheat oven to 450°F. Remove a thin slice from the bottom of each apple so it will stand. Remove a ¾-inch slice from the top. With a melon baller or grapefruit spoon, scoop out the center core of each apple. (Do not cut all the way through the bottom; leave a thick shell on the sides.)

2. In a small bowl, stir together cranberries or currants and brown sugar. Spoon ¼ of the mixture into each apple cavity. Set the apples in a small baking dish. Dot the top of each apple with ½ teaspoon butter. Pour cider or juice around the apples and cover the dish tightly with foil.

3. Bake for 30 minutes, or until the apples are almost tender. Uncover the pan and baste the apples with the pan juices. Bake uncovered for 10 minutes longer, basting once or twice more, or until the apples are tender and the juices are slightly reduced. Spoon the juices into the centers of the apples and serve warm.

Serves 4.

210 calories per serving: 1 gram protein, 2 grams fat (1 gram saturated fat), 50 grams carbohydrate; 26 mg sodium; 5 mg cholesterol.

✦**COOKING APPLES**

Often maligned as bland, a Golden Delicious can be surprisingly juicy and flavorful when eaten straight from the tree. This sweet apple holds its shape very well when cooked.

BAKED PEARS WITH GINGERSNAP CRUMBS

Bathed in honey-lemon syrup, this easy dessert is a comfort on a chilly night.

1. Preheat oven to 425°F. Crush gingersnaps between two pieces of plastic wrap or wax paper with a rolling pin or heavy pan. In a small bowl, whisk together honey, lemon juice and ginger.

2. Place pears, cut-side up, in a shallow 1-quart baking dish. Pour the honey syrup over the pears and sprinkle with the gingersnap crumbs. Bake for 10 minutes, baste with the syrup, then bake for 10 to 15 minutes longer, or until the pears are tender when pierced with a skewer and the syrup has thickened. Serve warm or at room temperature, with the sauce spooned over the pears.

Serves 4.

215 calories per serving: 1 gram protein, 1 gram fat (0 grams saturated fat), 54 grams carbohydrate; 45 mg sodium; 0 mg cholesterol.

4 gingersnaps

¼ cup honey

¼ cup fresh lemon juice (about 2 lemons)

½ teaspoon ground ginger

4 pears, peeled, halved and cored

PEARS ROYALE

Crème de cassis and white wine make up the fruity apéritif known as a kir royale. For this recipe, the black currant liqueur gives the pears a berry richness and a lush mahogany color.

Place oven rack in lower third of oven; preheat to 375°F. Set pear halves, cut-side down, in a baking dish. Pour crème de cassis and lemon juice over the top. Sprinkle with sugar and dot with butter. Bake, uncovered, about 45 minutes, basting occasionally with the pan juices, until the pears are tender and the juices have thickened slightly. Let cool briefly before serving.

Serves 4.

135 calories per serving: 1 gram protein, 2 grams fat (1 gram saturated fat), 36 grams carbohydrate; 156 mg sodium; 4 mg cholesterol.

4 small pears, peeled, halved and cored

⅓ cup crème de cassis

2 tablespoons fresh lemon juice

2 tablespoons sugar

½ tablespoon butter, cut into pieces

Fresh Grapefruit in Honey-Thyme Syrup

FRESH GRAPEFRUIT IN HONEY-THYME SYRUP

Here, the juice of the sectioned grapefruit is simmered down to an herb-scented sauce.

1. With a sharp knife, remove the skin and white pith from grapefruit and discard. Working over a bowl to catch the juice, cut the grapefruit segments from the surrounding membranes, letting them drop into the bowl. Squeeze the juice from the membranes into a small saucepan. Drain any juice from the bowl of segments into the pan as well.

2. With the back of a spoon, crush thyme leaves to release their fragrance. Add them to the saucepan, along with wine and honey. Simmer over medium-low heat until the sauce has reduced to ½ cup, 12 to 15 minutes. Strain the syrup into a bowl and let cool to room temperature.

3. To serve, arrange the grapefruit sections on individual dessert plates and drizzle with syrup. Garnish each plate with a thyme sprig.

Serves 4.

150 calories per serving: 1 gram protein, 0 grams fat, 40 grams carbohydrate; 5 mg sodium; 0 mg cholesterol.

3 **large** *or* 4 **small grapefruit, preferably pink** *or* **red**

2 **tablespoons fresh thyme leaves**

¼ **cup dry white wine**

¼ **cup honey**

Fresh thyme sprigs for garnish

◆ **CHOOSING GRAPEFRUIT**

Grapefruit flesh may be white, pink or ruby red; American consumers prefer pink and red over white, finding them sweeter, although all three varieties contain similar amounts of sugar. New red varieties to watch for include Flame, Star Ruby and Henderson.

CANDIED GRAPEFRUIT PEELS

A great cup of coffee and two or three of these bittersweet confections make a fine conclusion to a winter meal. The peels remain soft and full of flavor because they are made with the entire peel, including the white pith. The same technique works well with navel oranges.

3	pink grapefruit
2½	cups granulated sugar
2	teaspoons fresh lemon juice

1. Thoroughly scrub grapefruit with warm water and rub them dry. Divide the peel of each grapefruit into 4 segments by inserting a sharp knife just down to the flesh, making 4 equidistant longitudinal lines. Carefully peel back the quarters to remove the peel (including the white pith) in one piece. (Reserve the flesh for another use.) Following the contour of the peel, cut each quarter into 6 or 8 lengthwise strips.

2. Put the peels in a large saucepan and cover with cold water. Bring to a boil, blanch for 1 minute and drain. Repeat this step 2 more times.

3. In a large saucepan, combine 1½ cups of the sugar, lemon juice and the blanched peels. Cook over low heat, stirring occasionally, until the sugar dissolves. Simmer, stirring frequently, until nearly all the liquid has evaporated, 30 to 45 minutes. With tongs, transfer the peels to a wire rack and let cool for several hours.

4. Spread the remaining 1 cup sugar in a shallow dish and roll each strip of peel in the sugar, shaking off the excess. (*The peels can be stored in an airtight container, with wax paper between each layer, in a cool, dry place for up to 3 months.*)

Makes 6 to 7 dozen strips of candied peel.

30 calories each: 0 grams protein, 0 grams fat, 7 grams carbohydrate; 0 mg sodium; 0 mg cholesterol.

OLD-FASHIONED COMFORTS

Fools, buckles, cobblers and slumps are quaint names for nearly forgotten desserts. These were creations that cooks made with what was on hand, from the fresh berry confections of summer to the cozy rice puddings of winter. Old-fashioned

desserts have a goodness well worth preserving, except for one aspect. They tend to be high in fat: custards used to call for countless yolks, and full-fat cream was never an issue. Through judicious trimming, these recipes evoke the sweet memories of the past while putting forward a thoroughly enlightened nutrition profile.

RHUBARB & STRAWBERRY CRUMBLE

Serve warm, topped with a scoop of nonfat frozen yogurt.

FILLING

- 1   pound rhubarb, trimmed, and cut into ½-inch pieces (4 cups)
- 1   pint strawberries, hulled and quartered
- ½   cup white sugar
- 2   tablespoons all-purpose white flour

CRUMBLE TOPPING

- ½   cup rolled oats
- ½   cup all-purpose white flour
- ½   cup packed light brown sugar
- 1   tablespoon butter, softened
- 1   tablespoon canola oil
- 1   tablespoon cranberry *or* apple juice

TO MAKE FILLING:

Preheat oven to 375°F. In a large bowl, toss together rhubarb, strawberries, white sugar and flour. Transfer the mixture to a shallow 1½-quart baking dish or 9-inch deep-dish pie pan, pressing down on the fruit to form an even layer.

TO MAKE CRUMBLE TOPPING:

1. In a bowl, combine oats, flour, brown sugar, butter and oil; with a fork or your fingers, work the ingredients together until the mixture is crumbly. Stir in the cranberry or apple juice until the mixture is evenly moistened.

2. Distribute the topping mixture evenly over the fruit. Bake for 35 to 40 minutes, or until the fruit is bubbling and the topping is golden.

Serves 6.

270 calories per serving: 3 grams protein, 5 grams fat (1 gram saturated fat), 55 grams carbohydrate; 29 mg sodium; 5 mg cholesterol.

PEACHES & DUMPLINGS

The beauty of this dessert is you don't have to heat up the oven on a hot summer's evening.

1. In a bowl, whisk flour, 1½ teaspoons sugar, baking powder, baking soda and salt. In a small bowl, combine buttermilk, egg yolk and butter. Make a well in the center of the dry ingredients and pour in buttermilk mixture; stir gently to combine.

2. In a clean mixing bowl, beat egg white until soft peaks form. Fold into the batter. Set aside.

3. In a deep skillet or Dutch oven that is at least 10 inches wide, stir together 2½ cups water, the remaining 1 cup sugar and cinnamon. Add peaches and berries. Bring to a boil over medium heat, reduce the heat to low and simmer for 1 to 2 minutes, or just until tender. Do not overcook.

4. Drop the dumpling batter by spoonfuls over the simmering fruit, placing 5 spoonfuls around the outside edge and 1 in the center. Cover and cook for 8 to 10 minutes, or until the dumplings are firm to the touch. Serve warm.

Serves 6.

300 calories per serving: 5 grams protein, 3 grams fat (2 grams saturated fat), 66 grams carbohydrate; 297 mg sodium; 42 mg cholesterol.

1   cup all-purpose white flour

1   cup plus 1½ teaspoons sugar

1½   teaspoons baking powder

½   teaspoon baking soda

¼   teaspoon salt

½   cup plus 2 tablespoons buttermilk

1   large egg, separated

1   tablespoon butter, melted

    Pinch of cinnamon

4   large peaches, peeled (*see tip on page 13*), pitted and sliced (4 cups)

1   cup blackberries *or* blueberries

♦**SUBSTITUTION**

Tangy buttermilk is high in acid, which helps to tenderize cakes, biscuits and dumplings. If you don't have buttermilk in the refrigerator, you can substitute a mixture of half nonfat plain yogurt and half skim milk.

PEACH & TART CHERRY SHORTCAKES

Tender, not-too-sweet biscuits spill over with a luscious mixture of almond-scented fruits.

FRUIT FILLING

1	**pound tart cherries, pitted (2 cups)**
¼	**cup sugar**
1	**tablespoon fresh lemon juice**
1	**teaspoon cornstarch**
1	**tablespoon Amaretto *or* 1 tablespoon water mixed with ⅛ teaspoon almond extract**
4	**medium peaches (about 1½ pounds), peeled and sliced (*see tip on page 13*)**
1	**teaspoon grated lemon zest**

TO MAKE FRUIT FILLING:

1. In a saucepan, combine cherries, sugar and lemon juice. Heat over low heat, stirring occasionally, until the sugar dissolves. Simmer just until tender, about 5 minutes.

2. In a small bowl, stir together cornstarch and liqueur or water plus extract. Stir the mixture into the cherries and cook just until thickened. Remove from the heat and stir in peaches and lemon zest. Let cool. (*The filling can be made up to 4 hours in advance; cover by placing plastic wrap directly on the surface of the fruit to prevent browning, and refrigerate.*)

TO MAKE BISCUITS:

1. Preheat oven to 425°F. Lightly oil a baking sheet or coat it with nonstick cooking spray; set aside.

2. In a mixing bowl, stir together flour, ⅓ cup of the sugar, baking powder, baking soda and salt. Using a pastry cutter or your fingertips, cut butter into the dry ingredients until crumbly. In a small bowl, combine ¾ cup buttermilk, oil, vanilla and almond extracts. Make a well in the center of the dry ingredients and add the buttermilk mixture. With a fork, stir just until combined, adding additional buttermilk as needed to form a slightly sticky dough. Do not overmix.

3. Place the dough on a lightly floured surface and sprinkle with a little more flour. With your fingertips, gently pat the dough out into a 1-inch-thick round. With a 3- or 3½-inch round cutter, cut out biscuits and transfer them to the prepared baking sheet. Press together the scraps of dough and cut out additional biscuits (you should have 6). Brush the tops with milk. Scatter almonds over the tops and sprinkle with the remaining 1 tablespoon sugar.

4. Bake the biscuits for 10 to 15 minutes, or until golden. Transfer them to a wire rack and let cool slightly. With a serrated knife, split the biscuits. Set the bottoms on dessert plates; spoon on the fruit mixture, top with a scoop of frozen yogurt, if desired, and crown with the biscuit tops. Serve immediately.

Serves 6.

435 calories per serving: 9 grams protein, 10 grams fat (3 grams saturated fat), 79 grams carbohydrate; 359 mg sodium; 12 mg cholesterol.

BISCUITS

2¼ cups all-purpose white flour

⅓ cup sugar, plus 1 tablespoon for sprinkling over biscuits

1½ teaspoons baking powder

1 teaspoon baking soda

¼ teaspoon salt

2 tablespoons cold unsalted butter, cut into small pieces

¾-1 cup buttermilk

1 tablespoon canola oil

½ teaspoon pure vanilla extract

⅛ teaspoon pure almond extract

1 tablespoon skim milk

¼ cup sliced almonds

2 cups nonfat vanilla frozen yogurt (optional)

◆**ABOUT TART CHERRIES**

The season for tart cherries is short and sweet: it peaks in late July. Look for them at farmers' markets. Pitted tart cherries freeze well. You can use sweet cherries in the filling, but reduce the sugar to 2 tablespoons.

BERRY BUCKLE

An old Yankee dessert, a buckle usually includes berries, which are sprinkled over a cake batter and then baked.

TOPPING

- ⅓ cup rolled oats
- ⅓ cup all-purpose white flour
- ⅓ cup packed light brown sugar
- 1 tablespoon canola oil
- 1 tablespoon apple *or* cranberry juice
- ¼ teaspoon ground cinnamon

CAKE

- 1½ cups all-purpose white flour
- ½ cup granulated sugar
- 1 tablespoon baking powder
- ½ teaspoon salt
- 1 large egg
- 1 cup buttermilk
- 3 tablespoons canola oil
- 1 tablespoon grated lemon zest
- 1 teaspoon pure vanilla extract
- 1 cup fresh *or* frozen unsweetened raspberries, thawed
- 1 cup fresh *or* frozen unsweetened blackberries, thawed

TO PREPARE TOPPING:

Position oven rack in lower third of oven; preheat to 375°F. In a small bowl, stir together oats, flour, brown sugar, oil, fruit juice and cinnamon; work the mixture together with a fork or your fingers until it is evenly moistened. Set aside.

TO MAKE CAKE:

1. Lightly oil a 9-inch springform pan or coat it with nonstick cooking spray. In a large bowl, stir together flour, sugar, baking powder and salt. In another bowl, whisk together egg, buttermilk, oil, lemon zest and vanilla.

2. Add the egg mixture to the dry ingredients and stir with a rubber spatula just until blended. Spread the batter evenly in the prepared pan. Scatter the berries over the batter, then sprinkle with the reserved topping.

3. Bake for 40 to 45 minutes, or until the top feels firm when lightly pressed in the center. Remove the outer ring of the pan; serve warm or at room temperature.

Serves 10.

240 calories per serving: 4 grams protein, 7 grams fat (1 gram saturated fat), 41 grams carbohydrate; 240 mg sodium; 22 mg cholesterol.

♦**VARIATION**
Blueberries, particularly wild blueberries, would be wonderful too.

HUCKLEBERRY SLUMP

The slump has berries on the bottom and biscuit dough on top.

Preheat oven to 400°F. Lightly oil a 9-inch deep-dish pie pan or coat it with nonstick cooking spray.

TO MAKE FILLING:

Combine huckleberries or blueberries, sugar, cornstarch and lemon juice in a mixing bowl. Transfer to the prepared pan.

TO MAKE BISCUIT DOUGH:

1. In a mixing bowl, whisk together flour, ¼ cup sugar, baking powder, baking soda and salt. Using a pastry cutter or 2 forks, cut butter into the dry ingredients until crumbly. Stir in lemon zest. In a small bowl, whisk together the buttermilk and oil. Make a well in the center of the dry ingredients and pour the buttermilk into the center. With a fork, stir until just combined.

2. Turn the dough out onto a lightly floured surface. Roll or pat into a rough 8-inch circle. Gently lift the dough and set it on the berries. Use your fingers to pinch and patch together. (The dough is supposed to look rough.) Prick the dough in several places with the tines of a fork. Sprinkle the top with the remaining 1 teaspoon sugar.

3. Bake for 25 to 30 minutes, or until the fruit bubbles and the biscuit topping is golden brown. Transfer to a wire rack to cool. Serve warm or at room temperature.

Serves 8.

260 calories per serving: 4 grams protein, 5 grams fat (2 grams saturated fat), 53 grams carbohydrate; 282 mg sodium; 7 mg cholesterol.

FILLING

- 4 cups huckleberries *or* blueberries
- ⅔ cup sugar
- 1 tablespoon cornstarch
- 1 teaspoon fresh lemon juice

BISCUIT DOUGH

- 1½ cups all-purpose white flour
- ¼ cup plus 1 teaspoon sugar
- 1½ teaspoons baking powder
- 1 teaspoon baking soda
- ¼ teaspoon salt
- 1½ tablespoons cold unsalted butter
- 1 teaspoon grated lemon zest
- ¾ cup buttermilk
- 1 tablespoon canola oil

◆**VARIATION**

Blackberries or gooseberries are also excellent here.
Adjust the sugar according to the sweetness of the fruit.

SUMMER PUDDING

Although red currants are classic in summer pudding, they are difficult to come by. Other combinations of berries, such as raspberries or blueberries, can be used. Just be sure that at least half of the berries are red for the pudding to have the nicest color.

2 cups red currants

2 cups blackberries *or* loganberries

⅔ cup sugar

¼ cup pure strawberry jam *or* seedless raspberry jam

1 tablespoon crème de cassis *or* eau-de-vie de framboise (optional)

1 teaspoon fresh lemon juice

7-9 slices firm white sandwich bread, crusts trimmed

1 cup nonfat vanilla yogurt *or* Vanilla Cream (*page 182*)

1. In a large heavy saucepan, combine currants, blackberries or loganberries, sugar and 1 tablespoon water. Bring to a simmer, stirring. Simmer over medium-low heat for 2 minutes. Remove from the heat and stir in jam, liqueur, if using, and lemon juice. Let cool completely.

2. Line a 1-quart pudding basin or soufflé dish with plastic wrap, leaving a 4-inch overhang all around. Cut bread slices in half diagonally, then fit them in the bottom and sides of the dish, trimming further to fit snugly if needed. (You will have extra slices to be used for the top.)

3. Spoon the berry mixture into the bread-lined dish; trim the bread slices level with the top. Use the remaining bread slices to cover the top. Fold the plastic wrap over the pudding, then top with a plate slightly smaller than the diameter of the dish. Weight the plate with a heavy can. Refrigerate for at least 8 hours or up to 24 hours.

4. To serve, remove the weight and plate, then fold back the overlap of plastic wrap. Set a rimmed serving plate over the dish, then invert the pudding onto the plate. Remove the dish and plastic wrap. Carefully cut wedges with a serrated knife and serve each portion with a dollop of yogurt or Vanilla Cream.

Serves 6.

280 calories per serving: 5 grams protein, 1 gram fat (0 grams saturated fat), 63 grams carbohydrate; 183 mg sodium; 1 mg cholesterol.

◆**BERRY PICKING**

Pick berries in the morning, when the temperature of the fruit is not as high. Cool the berries as soon as possible.

Summer Pudding

TIRAMISÙ

This low-fat version of the ultra-high-fat Italian dessert is exceedingly good.

8   ounces ladyfingers (60 ladyfingers)

4   tablespoons brandy

1   tablespoon instant coffee granules, preferably espresso

1   cup plus 2 tablespoons sugar

3   large egg whites

¼   teaspoon cream of tartar

4   ounces mascarpone cheese (½ cup)

4   ounces reduced-fat cream cheese (½ cup), softened

    Chocolate shavings (*see tip on page 92*) for garnish

    Confectioners' sugar for garnish

1. If ladyfingers are the soft variety, toast them on a baking sheet in a 350°F oven for 6 to 8 minutes.

2. In a small bowl, stir together 3 tablespoons of the brandy, coffee granules and 1 cup water. Brush over the flat side of the ladyfingers. Set aside.

3. Bring about 1 inch of water to a simmer in a large saucepan. In a heatproof mixing bowl large enough to fit over the saucepan, combine sugar, egg whites, cream of tartar and 3 tablespoons of water. Set the bowl over the barely simmering water and beat with an electric mixer at low speed, moving the beaters around the bowl constantly, until an instant-read thermometer registers 140°F. (This will take 3 to 5 minutes.) Increase the mixer speed to high and continue beating over the heat for a full 3½ minutes. Remove the bowl from the heat and beat the meringue until cool, about 4 minutes. Set aside.

4. In a large bowl, beat mascarpone and cream cheese until creamy. Add about 1 cup of the meringue and the remaining 1 tablespoon brandy and beat until smooth, scraping down the sides of the bowl. Fold in the remaining meringue.

5. Line the bottom and sides of a 3-quart trifle bowl or soufflé dish with ladyfingers, the flat sides toward the center. Spoon in one-third of the filling and top with a layer of ladyfingers. Repeat with two more layers of filling and ladyfingers, arranging the final layer of ladyfingers decoratively over the top, trimming to fit, if necessary. Sprinkle with chocolate shavings. Cover and chill for at least 8 hours or overnight. Dust with confectioners' sugar and serve.

Serves 12.

200 calories per serving: 4 grams protein, 6 grams fat (1 gram saturated fat), 31 grams carbohydrate, 2 grams alcohol; 124 mg sodium; 16 mg cholesterol.

◆**STRETCHING HIGH-FAT INGREDIENTS**

The flavor of rich delights like mascarpone or cream cheese can be stretched by whipping them up with cooked meringue, which is totally fat-free.

CHERRY CLAFOUTIS

Originating in the countryside around the town of Limoges, France, a clafoutis is a baked fruit pudding.

1. Place rack in upper third of oven; preheat to 375°F. Lightly oil a 9-inch glass quiche dish or other small shallow baking dish, or coat it with nonstick cooking spray. Combine cherries and ⅓ cup of the sugar in the prepared dish. Bake for 20 minutes, or until the cherries are tender and very juicy.

2. Meanwhile, in a mixing bowl, whisk eggs, flour, vanilla and the remaining ¼ cup sugar until smooth. Whisk in evaporated skim milk.

3. Drain the juices from the cherries into a small bowl, holding back the fruit with a metal spatula. Reserve the juices. Redistribute the cherries over the bottom of the dish and pour in the egg mixture. Bake for 12 to 15 minutes, or until puffed and set. Dust with confectioners' sugar and serve immediately, with the reserved cherry juices spooned over the top.

Serves 4.

225 calories per serving: 6 grams protein, 3 grams fat (1 gram saturated fat), 46 grams carbohydrate; 57 mg sodium; 107 mg cholesterol.

1	**pound tart cherries, pitted**
⅓	**cup plus ¼ cup sugar**
2	**large eggs**
2	**tablespoons all-purpose white flour**
1½	**teaspoons pure vanilla extract**
⅓	**cup evaporated skim milk** **Confectioners' sugar for dusting**

◆ **CHERRY STAINS**
If your hands are stained from pitting cherries, a little lemon juice will remove the stains.

Pear-Cranberry Sampler

PEAR-CRANBERRY SAMPLER

Even easier to make than a classic cobbler, this comforting warm fruit dessert uses a French-toast topping.

¼ cup plus 3 tablespoons sugar

1 tablespoon cornstarch

5 ripe pears, cored, peeled and chopped (4 cups)

1 cup fresh *or* frozen cranberries

⅓ cup low-fat milk

2 large eggs

1 teaspoon pure vanilla extract

6 slices firm white bread, crusts trimmed

¼ teaspoon freshly grated nutmeg

1. Preheat oven to 400°F. In an 8-inch square baking dish, stir together ¼ cup of the sugar and cornstarch. Add pears and cranberries and stir until well combined. Place in the oven to bake for 20 minutes, stirring midway, or until the fruit is tender and the juices have begun to thicken.

2. Meanwhile, in a large shallow dish, whisk together milk, eggs and vanilla. Cut each bread slice in half diagonally, and soak in the egg-milk mixture, carefully turning the slices for even soaking.

3. Remove the fruit from the oven and arrange the bread in rows on top of the fruit. Combine nutmeg and the remaining 3 tablespoons sugar; sprinkle evenly over the bread. Bake for 20 minutes more, or until the fruit is bubbling and the bread is golden. Serve immediately.

Serves 6.

260 calories per serving: 5 grams protein, 3 grams fat (1 gram saturated fat), 55 grams carbohydrate; 147 mg sodium; 72 mg cholesterol.

LEMON MOUSSE

This velvety mousse is the perfect answer when a hearty meal needs a light finale.

1. Bring about 1 inch of water to a simmer in a large saucepan. In a heatproof mixing bowl large enough to fit over the saucepan, combine ⅔ cup sugar, egg whites, cream of tartar and 3 tablespoons of water. Set the bowl over the barely simmering water and beat with an electric mixer at low speed, moving the beaters around the bowl constantly, until an instant-read thermometer registers 140°F. (This will take 3 to 5 minutes.) Increase the mixer speed to high and continue beating over the heat for a full 3½ minutes. Remove the bowl from the heat and beat the meringue until cool, about 4 minutes. Set aside.

2. Place 3 tablespoons cold water in a small bowl. If using food coloring, add about 3 drops to the water. Sprinkle in gelatin and let stand for 2 minutes to soften. Dissolve the softened gelatin in the microwave or over the simmering water. Set aside.

3. In another heatproof bowl large enough to fit over the saucepan of simmering water, combine whole eggs, lemon juice, lemon zest and the remaining ¼ cup sugar. Set the bowl over the barely simmering water and whisk slowly and constantly until the mixture thickens and reaches 160°F. Remove the bowl from the heat and whisk in the dissolved gelatin. Let cool for 20 minutes.

4. Beat the whipping cream in a chilled bowl until soft peaks form. Set aside.

5. Whisk about one-fourth of the meringue into the cooled lemon mixture to lighten it. Add the remaining meringue and use a whisk to incorporate it with a folding motion. With a rubber spatula, fold in the whipped cream.

6. Divide the mousse among 6 dessert dishes or stemmed glasses. Cover loosely and refrigerate until set, about 3 hours. (*The mousse can be stored, covered, in the refrigerator for up to 2 days.*) Garnish with lemon slices before serving.

Serves 6.

185 calories per serving: 5 grams protein, 5 grams fat (2 grams saturated fat), 33 grams carbohydrate; 53 mg sodium; 82 mg cholesterol.

⅔ cup plus ¼ cup sugar
3 large egg whites
½ teaspoon cream of tartar
  Yellow food coloring (optional)
1 teaspoon unflavored gelatin
2 large eggs
½ cup fresh lemon juice
1 tablespoon grated lemon zest
¼ cup whipping cream
  Lemon slices for garnish

◆ **SAFE MERINGUE**
Fluffy meringue is a great tool for adding fat-free lightness to desserts. Although the risk of salmonella contamination in raw egg whites is very low, we do recommend using a cooked meringue.

Egg whites must be heated to 140°F and maintained at that temperature for a full 3½ minutes to destroy any bacteria. You will need an instant-read thermometer to ensure that the proper temperature is reached.

BAKED RICE PUDDING

Plump golden raisins dot these creamy individual puddings.

4½ cups low-fat milk

¾ cup sugar

⅔ cup medium-grain rice, such as arborio

½ cup golden raisins

2 large eggs

1 tablespoon rum, brandy *or* orange juice

1 teaspoon grated orange zest

1 teaspoon pure vanilla extract

1. In a large heavy saucepan, bring milk to a simmer, stirring occasionally to prevent scorching. Add sugar and rice and simmer over low heat, stirring occasionally, until the rice is very tender, about 40 minutes. Stir in raisins and transfer to a bowl to cool; stir occasionally.

2. Preheat oven to 325°F. Lightly coat eight 6-ounce custard cups or ramekins with nonstick cooking spray. In a small bowl, whisk eggs, rum, brandy or orange juice, orange zest and vanilla until well blended; stir into the cooled rice. Spoon into the prepared custard cups.

3. Bake for 25 to 30 minutes, or until the filling is just set. Cool on a wire rack for 10 minutes; run a knife around the insides of the cups and invert onto dessert plates. Serve warm.

Serves 8.

235 calories per serving: 7 grams protein, 3 grams fat (1 gram saturated fat), 45 grams carbohydrate; 86 mg sodium; 59 mg cholesterol.

LEMON PUDDING

A perennial favorite, this version has been lightened by using low-fat milk and fewer egg yolks.

½ cup sugar

1 large egg

1½ tablespoons butter, softened

2 teaspoons grated lemon zest

3 tablespoons all-purpose white flour

1 cup low-fat milk

¼ cup fresh lemon juice

3 large egg whites
Confectioners' sugar for dusting

1. Preheat oven to 350°F. Lightly oil four 6-ounce custard cups or ramekins or coat them with nonstick cooking spray.

2. In a mixing bowl, beat sugar, whole egg, butter and lemon zest with an electric mixer until the mixture is thick and pale, about 3 minutes. Add flour and beat until smooth. Mix in milk and lemon juice.

3. In a clean mixing bowl using clean beaters, beat egg whites until stiff but not dry. Gently fold the whites into the egg-sugar mixture until completely incorporated. Spoon into the prepared cups. Set them in a shallow baking dish and add enough hot water to come two-thirds of the way up the sides. Bake for 30 minutes, or until browned and set. Serve warm or chilled, dusted with confectioners' sugar.

Serves 4.

210 calories per serving: 7 grams protein, 6 grams fat (3 grams saturated fat), 33 grams carbohydrate; 132 mg sodium; 67 mg cholesterol.

CAPPUCCINO BREAD PUDDING

A richly flavored version of an old favorite, drizzled with warm caramel sauce.

1. Lightly oil a 1½- to 2-quart shallow baking dish or coat it with non-stick cooking spray.

2. In a saucepan, simmer coffee over low heat until it is reduced to ½ cup, 7 to 8 minutes; let cool to lukewarm.

3. In a mixing bowl, whisk eggs, brown sugar and cinnamon until smooth. Whisk in evaporated skim milk, then add the lukewarm coffee.

4. Arrange bread cubes in an even layer in the prepared baking dish. Pour the milk mixture evenly over the bread. Let soak for 30 minutes. Meanwhile, preheat oven to 325°F.

5. Sprinkle almonds over the top of the pudding and bake for 25 minutes. Increase oven temperature to 425° and bake for 5 to 8 minutes longer, or until the top is browned and the nuts are toasted. Let stand for 10 minutes.

TO MAKE CARAMEL SAUCE:

1. In a small heavy saucepan, combine sugar, lemon juice and ½ cup water. Bring to a boil over medium-high heat, stirring to dissolve the sugar. Cook, without stirring, until the syrup turns deep amber, 10 to 15 minutes. Remove the caramel from the heat and let cool for 2 minutes. Whisk in butter until it is incorporated, then gradually whisk in evaporated skim milk. Return to low heat and stir until the caramel has dissolved completely. Whisk in vanilla. Let cool slightly before serving.

2. To serve, dust the top of the pudding with confectioners' sugar and pass the warm caramel sauce alongside.

Serves 6.

395 calories per serving: 13 grams protein, 7 grams fat (2 grams saturated fat), 71 grams carbohydrate; 313 mg sodium; 80 mg cholesterol.

1   cup strong brewed coffee, preferably espresso

2   large eggs

⅓   cup packed light brown sugar

½   teaspoon ground cinnamon

1½   cups evaporated skim milk (one 12-ounce can)

4   cups cubed firm white bread, crusts removed (about 8 slices)

¼   cup sliced almonds
    Confectioners' sugar for dusting

CARAMEL SAUCE

1   cup white sugar

1   teaspoon lemon juice

1   tablespoon butter

¾   cup evaporated skim milk

½   teaspoon pure vanilla extract

SOUFFLÉED SEMOLINA PUDDING

Unlike many dessert soufflés, this pudding can sit without falling. Old recipes often call for unmolding it after baking, but its golden surface looks so good that you can serve it right from the baking dish.

½ cup raisins

3 tablespoons grappa *or* brandy

2 cups skim milk

½ cup semolina flour (*see page 8*)

2 large eggs, separated

½ cup sugar, plus more for preparing dish

1 tablespoon grated lemon zest

1½ teaspoons pure vanilla extract

1 large egg white
   Pinch of salt

◆INGREDIENT NOTE

Grappa is a clear brandy distilled from the skins and stems of grapes.

1. Soak raisins in grappa or brandy for 30 to 40 minutes, or until softened, stirring occasionally. Set aside.

2. In a heavy saucepan, bring milk to a boil; reduce the heat to low. Whisking constantly, add semolina in a thin stream. Continue to cook, whisking frequently, for 5 to 8 minutes, or until the mixture is thick and almost moves together as a mass. Remove from the heat and whisk in egg yolks, one at a time. Whisk in ¼ cup of the sugar, lemon zest and vanilla.

3. Transfer to a bowl and cool to lukewarm, whisking occasionally, about 10 minutes. Stir the raisins and their liquid into the semolina mixture.

4. Place rack in lower third of oven; preheat to 350°F. Lightly oil a 1½-quart soufflé dish or coat it with nonstick cooking spray. Sprinkle the dish with sugar, tapping out the excess, and set aside.

5. In a clean mixing bowl, beat the 3 egg whites until frothy, add salt and continue to beat until soft peaks form. Gradually add the remaining ¼ cup sugar and beat until stiff but not dry. Stir one-third of the beaten whites into the semolina mixture. Fold in the remaining whites just until combined. Carefully pour into the soufflé dish.

6. Place the soufflé dish in a baking dish and set on the oven rack. Pour hot water into the baking dish until it reaches 1½ inches up the side of the soufflé dish. Bake for 1 hour and 40 minutes to 1 hour and 50 minutes, or until puffed, golden and set. Carefully remove the dish from the water and cool on a wire rack for 5 minutes before serving.

Serves 6.

210 calories per serving: 7 grams protein, 2 grams fat (1 gram saturated fat), 38 grams carbohydrate; 74 mg sodium; 72 mg cholesterol.

RUM-RAISIN BREAD PUDDING

Inspired by one of our favorite flavors of ice cream, we developed this very low-fat treat.

1. Preheat oven to 350°F. Put raisins in a small bowl, sprinkle with rum or brandy and set aside to soak for 10 minutes. Lightly oil an 8-inch square baking dish or coat it with nonstick cooking spray. Spread bread in the dish in an even layer.

2. In a mixing bowl, whisk eggs. Add evaporated skim milk, brown sugar, vanilla and nutmeg; whisk until the sugar dissolves. Stir in rum-soaked raisins. Pour the mixture over the bread. With a fork, mix in any unsoaked bread pieces. Let stand for 10 minutes.

3. Bake for 35 to 40 minutes, or until puffed and set in the center. Serve warm, with a scoop of frozen yogurt on top.

Serves 6.

365 calories per serving: 11 grams protein, 3 grams fat (1 gram saturated fat), 72 grams carbohydrate; 272 mg sodium; 73 mg cholesterol.

½ cup raisins

2 tablespoons rum *or* brandy

4 slices whole-wheat bread, torn into small pieces

2 large eggs

1½ cups evaporated skim milk (one 12-ounce can)

¾ cup packed light brown sugar

1 tablespoon pure vanilla extract

½ teaspoon freshly grated nutmeg

3 cups nonfat vanilla frozen yogurt

◆**GRATING NUTMEG**

Use a nutmeg grater or the tiniest holes of a box grater to grate whole nutmeg. (See page 10.)

FLAN

A fairly firm flan with a sublime flavor and silky texture.

½ cup sugar

2 large eggs

3 large egg whites

1 14-ounce can nonfat *or* low-fat sweetened condensed milk

1½ cups skim milk

1 tablespoon pure vanilla extract

1. Preheat oven to 325°F. In a small heavy saucepan, combine sugar with ¼ cup water. Bring to a simmer over low heat, stirring occasionally. Increase the heat to medium-high and cook, without stirring, until the syrup turns a deep amber color, about 5 minutes. (Swirl the pan if the syrup is coloring unevenly.) Immediately pour the syrup into a 1½- or 2-quart soufflé dish or casserole and carefully tilt the dish so that the caramel coats halfway up the side.

2. In a large bowl, whisk together eggs and egg whites. Add condensed milk, skim milk and vanilla, blending well.

3. Pour the mixture through a fine strainer into the caramel-coated dish. Set the dish in a larger shallow pan, such as a roasting pan. Pour enough hot water into the larger pan so it comes halfway up the side of the custard dish. Bake for 60 to 70 minutes, or until the custard is set around the edges but still wobbly in the center.

4. Remove the dish from its water bath to a rack to cool to room temperature. Then cover and refrigerate for at least 4 hours or overnight. To serve, run a knife around the inside of the dish and invert the flan onto a plate.

Serves 6.

310 calories per serving: 11 grams protein, 2 grams fat (1 gram saturated fat), 61 grams carbohydrate; 148 mg sodium; 80 mg cholesterol.

♦**INGREDIENT NOTE**

Sweetened condensed milk was developed in 1853 as a way to keep milk from spoiling. Today, health-conscious cooks use the recently developed low-fat and nonfat versions of the product for puddings and pie fillings—wherever a creamy sweetness is desired.

Flan

APRICOT FOOL

The traditional fruit for a fool is the gooseberry. But tart dried apricots work admirably as well,
as does substituting yogurt for most of the usual cream.

1½   cups nonfat plain yogurt

½   pound dried apricots
      (about 2 cups)

¾   cup granulated sugar

½   cup confectioners' sugar

¼   cup Amaretto *or* ¼ cup
      fresh orange juice plus ½
      teaspoon pure almond
      extract

1   teaspoon pure vanilla
      extract

⅓   cup whipping cream

¼   cup sliced almonds

1. Line a sieve with cheesecloth or a coffee filter and set it over a bowl. Spoon in yogurt and let it drain in the refrigerator for 1 hour, or until reduced to 1 cup.

2. Meanwhile, in a heavy saucepan, combine apricots, granulated sugar and 2½ cups water. Bring to a boil over medium heat. Cover and reduce heat to low; simmer until apricots are tender, about 10 minutes. With a slotted spoon, remove 12 apricot halves, chop coarsely and set aside. Transfer the remaining apricots and the cooking liquid to a food processor or blender and puree until smooth. Place in a bowl, cover and refrigerate for 20 to 30 minutes, or until cool but not cold.

3. In a bowl, stir together the cooled apricot puree, drained yogurt, chopped apricots, confectioners' sugar, Amaretto (or orange juice plus almond extract) and vanilla. In a separate bowl, whip cream until stiff. Fold into the apricot mixture. Spoon into a serving bowl or individual dishes or parfait glasses. Cover and refrigerate until chilled, at least 1 hour. (*The recipe can be prepared ahead and stored, covered, in the refrigerator for up to 2 days.*)

4. Preheat oven to 350°F. Spread almonds in a pie pan and toast for 5 to 10 minutes, or until golden. Let cool. Sprinkle the almonds over the fool and serve.

Serves 6.

350 calories per serving: 6 grams protein, 7 grams fat (3 grams saturated fat), 65 grams carbohydrate; 53 mg sodium; 16 mg cholesterol.

APPLE CHARLOTTES

Crisp, golden little versions of the classic French dessert. If you like, serve them with Vanilla Custard Sauce (page 182).

1. Preheat oven to 375°F. Lightly coat four 6-ounce custard cups with nonstick cooking spray. Sprinkle 1 teaspoon sugar in each cup and swirl to coat the inside.

2. Lay 4 slices of bread on a work surface. With a cookie cutter or paring knife, cut out 4 circles of bread, each just large enough to fit in the bottom of a custard cup. Trim the crusts from the 6 remaining slices and cut each slice into 4 squares. Line the inside of each cup with the squares, slightly overlapping them. Set aside.

3. In a large saucepan, toss diced apples with lemon juice. Add raisins, sugar and lemon zest and cook, stirring, over medium-high heat until the mixture comes to a simmer.

4. In a small bowl, whisk flour and 2 tablespoons water until smooth; stir into the apple mixture and cook, stirring, until the mixture thickens. Remove from the heat. Crack the egg into a small bowl and whisk until frothy. Stir some of the hot apples into the egg, then stir the mixture back into the saucepan. Return the pan to the stovetop; stir over low heat until the egg sets and the filling has thickened, about 2 minutes. Remove from the heat and stir in butter and vanilla.

5. Spoon the filling into the bread-lined custard cups. With a rubber spatula, press the filling well down into the cups, smoothing the top. Transfer to a baking sheet and bake for 20 to 25 minutes, or until the bread is golden on the sides and bottom. Run a knife around the insides of the cups and invert onto dessert plates. Serve warm.

Serves 4.

370 calories per serving: 7 grams protein, 5 grams fat (2 grams saturated fat), 78 grams carbohydrate; 279 mg sodium; 58 mg cholesterol.

4 teaspoons sugar

10 slices thin-sliced firm white bread (such as Pepperidge Farm)

2½ cups diced peeled cooking apples, such as Rome Beauty, Cortland, Northern Spy *or* Golden Delicious (about 3 small apples)

2 tablespoons fresh lemon juice

½ cup golden raisins

½ cup sugar

2 teaspoons grated lemon zest

1 tablespoon all-purpose white flour

1 large egg

2 teaspoons butter

½ teaspoon pure vanilla extract

MANGO-CRANBERRY COBBLER

An unlikely combination of fruits in a dessert from Texas chef Stephan Pyles.

4	cups cranberries
1⅓	cups sugar
2	tablespoons grated orange zest
2	tablespoons unsalted butter
2	tablespoons canola oil
1	egg, lightly beaten
1½	cups all-purpose white flour
1	tablespoon baking powder
¾	cup buttermilk
3	ripe mangoes, peeled, pitted and cubed (*see tip on page 59*)

1. Preheat oven to 350°F. Lightly oil an 8-by-12-inch or 7-by-11-inch baking pan or coat it with nonstick cooking spray; set aside.

2. In a food processor, pulse cranberries until coarsely chopped. Place in a large mixing bowl with 1 cup of the sugar and orange zest. Stir to combine. Let stand for 15 minutes, stirring occasionally.

3. In a mixing bowl, beat butter, oil and the remaining ⅓ cup sugar with an electric mixer until light and fluffy. Add egg and mix well. Sift flour and baking powder together and add to the butter mixture alternately with buttermilk.

4. Spread mangoes and the reserved cranberry mixture evenly in the prepared baking pan. Spoon the cobbler dough over the fruit, covering it completely. Bake for 40 to 50 minutes, or until the topping is browned and the fruit mixture is bubbling. Remove from the oven and let stand for 5 to 10 minutes before serving. (*The cobbler can be assembled 1 hour ahead and refrigerated until you are ready to bake it.*)

Serves 8.

360 calories per serving: 5 grams protein, 8 grams fat (2 grams saturated fat), 72 grams carbohydrate; 187 mg sodium; 35 mg cholesterol.

◆**JUDGING MANGOES**

Ripe mangoes are soft, like ripe avocados. The fruit should smell sweet. Color is not an indication of ripeness. Mangoes are available year-round.

IRRESISTIBLE CHOCOLATE

I t's the quintessential indulgence—and an absolute necessity for many of us. But most chocolate desserts are quintessentially rich, because chocolate itself is high in fat and it goes so well with butter, cream and eggs. In the EATING WELL Test Kitchen, chocolate desserts receive special attention: our goal is to create recipes that give this marvelous flavor its full, deep expression, but with a fraction of the fat. Chocolate mousse, fudge cake, chocolate cheesecake and 10 more chocolate classics have been revamped with enticing results.

In many recipes, cocoa powder replaces chocolate: by weight, cocoa has 60 percent less fat than unsweetened chocolate. Many of these recipes specify Dutch-process cocoa, which has a deeper flavor than American-style cocoa and imparts a darker color as well.

CHOCOLATE MOUSSE À L'ORANGE

Enjoy this low-fat mousse spoonful by lovin' spoonful: it is just as luscious as its full-fat cousin.

¾ cup low-fat milk

6 2-inch-long strips of orange zest

1 teaspoon unflavored gelatin

2 tablespoons Grand Marnier *or* other orange liqueur

1 large egg

1 cup packed light brown sugar

⅔ cup unsweetened cocoa powder, preferably Dutch-process

2 ounces bittersweet (*not* unsweetened) chocolate, chopped

2 teaspoons pure vanilla extract

4 large egg whites

½ teaspoon cream of tartar

Chocolate shavings (optional)

1. In a small saucepan, heat milk and orange zest until steaming. Remove from the heat and let steep for 10 minutes. Discard the orange zest. In a small bowl, sprinkle gelatin over Grand Marnier; let stand until softened, 1 minute or longer.

2. In another saucepan, whisk together whole egg, ¼ cup of the brown sugar, cocoa and the infused milk until smooth. Cook over low heat, whisking constantly, until thickened, about 5 minutes. Remove from the heat and add the softened gelatin mixture, stirring until the gelatin has dissolved. Then add chocolate and vanilla; stir until the chocolate has melted. Set aside to cool to room temperature, about 30 minutes.

3. Bring about 1 inch of water to a simmer in a wide saucepan. In a heatproof bowl large enough to fit over the saucepan, combine egg whites, cream of tartar, 3 tablespoons water and the remaining ¾ cup brown sugar. Set the bowl over the barely simmering water and beat with an electric mixer at low speed, moving the beaters around constantly, until an instant-read thermometer registers 140°F. (This will take 3 to 5 minutes.) Increase the mixer speed to high and continue beating over the heat for a full 3½ minutes. Remove the bowl from the heat and beat the meringue until cool, 4 to 5 minutes longer.

4. Whisk one-fourth of the meringue into the chocolate mixture until smooth. With a rubber spatula, fold the chocolate mixture back into the remaining meringue until completely incorporated. Spoon the mousse into 6 dessert glasses and chill until set, about 3 hours. (*The mousse can be stored, covered, in the refrigerator for up to 2 days.*) Garnish each mousse with chocolate shavings, if using, and serve.

Serves 6.

250 calories per serving: 6 grams protein, 4 grams fat (0 grams saturated fat), 45 grams carbohydrate; 75 mg sodium; 37 mg cholesterol.

◆**CHOCOLATE SHAVINGS**
Place a block of chocolate (2 ounces or larger) on wax paper and microwave, uncovered, at medium-low (30 percent) power for 15 seconds. Turn chocolate block over and microwave for 10 to 15 seconds longer, or just until the chocolate has softened slightly but has not started to melt. Use a vegetable peeler to shave off curls. (If the chocolate is too hard to shave easily, warm it again.)

Chocolate Mousse à l'Orange

CHOCOLATE SOUFFLÉ

One word describes this soufflé: superb. The deep chocolate flavor comes from cocoa, with a small amount of unsweetened chocolate to intensify it. The result is surprisingly low in fat. Serve with Brandied Cherry Sauce (page 179) or simply on its own.

⅔ cup unsweetened cocoa powder, preferably Dutch-process

¾ cup sugar, plus extra for preparing soufflé dish(es)

4 teaspoons cornstarch

⅛ teaspoon ground cinnamon

1 cup skim milk

2 teaspoons pure vanilla extract

7 large egg whites, at room temperature

¼ teaspoon cream of tartar

Pinch of salt

½ ounce unsweetened chocolate, grated

Confectioners' sugar for dusting

1. In a small heavy saucepan, blend cocoa, ¼ cup of the sugar, cornstarch and cinnamon. Whisk in milk. Bring to a boil over medium heat, whisking constantly. Continue stirring and cook for 1 minute, or until thickened. Remove from the heat and stir in vanilla. Let cool to room temperature.

2. Position rack in the lower third of the oven; preheat to 350°F. Lightly oil a 2-quart soufflé dish or six 1½-cup individual soufflé dishes or coat them with nonstick cooking spray. Sprinkle with a little sugar and tap out the excess.

3. In a large, grease-free mixing bowl, beat egg whites with an electric mixer on medium speed until foamy and opaque. Add cream of tartar and salt; gradually increase speed to high and beat until soft peaks form. Gradually add the remaining ½ cup sugar and beat until stiff, but not dry, peaks form.

4. Stir the cocoa mixture well. Whisk about one-fourth of the beaten egg whites into the cocoa mixture to lighten it. Sprinkle in the grated chocolate and, using a rubber spatula, fold the cocoa mixture back into the remaining whites. Turn into the prepared dish or dishes and smooth the top with the spatula.

5. Place in a deep baking dish or roasting pan. Fill the pan with hot water to come one-third of the way up the side of the dish or dishes. Bake until puffed and the top feels firm to the touch, about 25 minutes for individual soufflés or about 40 minutes for a large soufflé. Dust with confectioners' sugar and serve immediately.

Serves 6.

155 calories per serving: 6 grams protein, 2 grams fat (0 grams saturated fat), 30 grams carbohydrate; 86 mg sodium; 1 mg cholesterol.

CHOCOLATE SHORTCAKES

Delicate chocolate shortcakes are a perfect pairing with early summer's strawberries. The biscuit dough for these shortcakes is especially quick because it doesn't need to be patted or rolled.

TO MAKE FILLING:

Line a sieve with cheesecloth or a coffee filter and set it over a bowl. Spoon in yogurt and let it drain in the refrigerator for 30 to 60 minutes. In a bowl, toss strawberries with sugar. Let stand at room temperature for 20 to 30 minutes, stirring occasionally, until the strawberries have begun to give off juice.

TO MAKE BISCUITS:

1. Preheat oven to 400°F. Line a baking sheet with parchment paper or coat it with nonstick cooking spray.

2. In a mixing bowl, whisk together flour, cocoa, sugar, baking powder, baking soda and salt. Using a pastry cutter or your fingertips, cut butter and cream cheese into the dry ingredients until crumbly. Make a well in the center and add buttermilk, stirring with a fork until evenly moistened. Drop 4 mounds of batter, about 2 inches apart, onto the prepared baking sheet. Shape the mounds into 3-inch circles and bake for 10 to 12 minutes, or until the tops spring back when touched lightly. Transfer the biscuits to a wire rack and let cool slightly.

TO ASSEMBLE SHORTCAKES:

With a serrated knife, slice the biscuits in half crosswise. Set the bottoms on dessert plates. Spoon the strawberries and their juice over the biscuits and add a dollop of the drained yogurt. Crown with the biscuit tops, dust with confectioners' sugar and serve.

Serves 4.

300 calories per serving: 7 grams protein, 6 grams fat (3 grams saturated fat), 57 grams carbohydrate; 428 mg sodium; 15 mg cholesterol.

FILLING

- 1 cup low-fat vanilla yogurt
- 1 pint strawberries, hulled and sliced
- 3 tablespoons sugar

CHOCOLATE BISCUITS

- ⅔ cup all-purpose white flour
- ⅓ cup unsweetened cocoa powder
- ⅓ cup sugar
- 1½ teaspoons baking powder
- ¼ teaspoon baking soda
- ¼ teaspoon salt
- 1½ tablespoons butter
- 1½ tablespoons reduced-fat cream cheese
- ½ cup buttermilk
  Confectioners' sugar for dusting

◆**FAT-CUTTING TIP**

Low-fat or nonfat vanilla yogurt drained briefly through cheesecloth or a coffee filter makes a quick and healthy dessert topping.

Chocolate Madeleines

CHOCOLATE MADELEINES

French novelist and notorious shut-in Marcel Proust was passionate about the plump little cakelike cookies called madeleines. Perhaps the aroma of this chocolate version baking in the oven would have drawn him out of his room.

1. Preheat oven to 400°F. Brush a madeleine pan with oil or coat it with nonstick cooking spray. Dust with flour, tapping out the excess; set aside. (*Alternatively, if you do not have a madeleine pan, coat and flour 18 small fluted tartlet tins.*)

2. Place whole egg and egg white in a mixing bowl and set the bowl in a larger pan of hot water to warm while you prepare the remaining ingredients. Stir the eggs occasionally.

3. Sift flour, cocoa, baking powder, baking soda and salt into a bowl; set aside. Combine buttermilk and oil and set aside.

4. Take the egg bowl off the water, add sugar and beat with an electric mixer on high speed until the mixture is thickened and pale, about 5 minutes. (The beaters should leave a ribbon trail when lifted.) Blend in vanilla and coffee or orange zest. With a rubber spatula, alternately fold the dry ingredients and the buttermilk mixture into the egg mixture, making 3 additions of dry ingredients and 2 additions of liquid.

5. Drop the batter by tablespoonfuls into the prepared pan, filling each depression about three-fourths full; you will use about half of the batter. Bake for 12 to 15 minutes, or until the tops of the madeleines spring back when touched lightly. Immediately loosen the cakes from the pan and invert onto a wire rack to cool. Clean and prepare the pan as above and repeat with the remaining batter. (*The madeleines are best eaten the day they are baked, but they can be wrapped and frozen for up to 1 month.*)

6. If decorating with chocolate, melt it in a small bowl set over a pan of barely simmering water. Drizzle over the scalloped side of the madeleines. Alternatively, dust the madeleines with confectioners' sugar.

Makes about 2 dozen madeleines.

70 calories per madeleine: 1 gram protein, 2 grams fat (0 grams saturated fat), 11 grams carbohydrate; 70 mg sodium; 9 mg cholesterol.

1 large egg
1 large egg white
1 cup all-purpose white flour
¼ cup unsweetened cocoa powder, preferably Dutch-process
1½ teaspoons baking powder
½ teaspoon baking soda
¼ teaspoon salt
½ cup buttermilk
3 tablespoons canola oil
¾ cup sugar
1 teaspoon pure vanilla extract
1 teaspoon instant coffee granules *or* 2 teaspoons grated orange zest
1 ounce bittersweet (*not* unsweetened) chocolate *or* confectioners' sugar for decoration

◆**CHOCOLATE TIMESAVER**

An easy way to decorate with thin lines of chocolate is to melt the chocolate in a plastic bag in the microwave. Then snip a small hole in one corner of the bag and quickly squeeze out lines of chocolate over the dessert.

COCOA ROULADE
WITH RASPBERRY CREAM

This light sponge cake is rolled around a luxurious raspberry meringue. Serve drizzled with Raspberry-Chocolate Sauce (page 178), if desired, and a scattering of additional berries.

CAKE

⅓ cup unsweetened cocoa powder, plus additional for dusting the pan and cake

⅓ cup sifted cake flour

1 teaspoon baking powder

¼ teaspoon salt

2 large eggs

½ cup sugar

1½ teaspoons pure vanilla extract

3 large egg whites

TO MAKE CAKE:

1. Preheat oven to 350°F. Lightly oil a 10-by-15-inch baking sheet with sides; line the bottom with parchment or wax paper and oil or spray it again. Dust the paper with cocoa, tapping off the excess. Set aside.

2. In a bowl, whisk together cocoa, flour, baking powder and salt. In a mixing bowl, beat whole eggs and ¼ cup of the sugar with an electric mixer until thickened and pale, about 5 minutes. Beat in vanilla.

3. In a large clean bowl with clean beaters, beat egg whites until soft peaks form. Gradually beat in the remaining ¼ cup sugar, beating until stiff and glossy. Whisk one-fourth of the beaten whites into the whole-egg mixture. Sprinkle half of the cocoa mixture over the top and fold in with a rubber spatula just until blended. Fold in the remaining beaten whites, then the remaining cocoa mixture.

4. Spoon the batter into the prepared pan, spreading it to the edges. Bake for 10 to 15 minutes, or until the top springs back when lightly touched. (Do not overbake or the cake will crack when rolled.) While the cake is baking, place a clean kitchen towel on the work surface. Cover it with parchment or wax paper, spray the paper with nonstick cooking spray and dust lightly with cocoa.

5. Once the cake is done, loosen the edges and invert the cake onto the cocoa-dusted paper. Peel the paper from the top of the cake. Using a serrated knife, trim the edges of the cake, then quickly roll up the cake in the paper-lined towel, starting at a short end. Set the rolled cake, seam-side down, on a rack to cool.

TO MAKE FILLING:

1. Bring about 1 inch of water to a simmer in a large saucepan. Put egg whites, sugar, cream of tartar and 2 tablespoons water in a heatproof bowl that will fit over the pan. Set the bowl over the simmering water and beat with an electric mixer at low speed, moving the beaters around the bowl constantly, until an instant-read thermometer registers 140°F, 3 to 5 minutes. Increase the mixer speed to high and continue beating for a full 3½ minutes. Remove the bowl from the heat and beat the meringue until cool, about 4 minutes.

2. In a small saucepan, sprinkle gelatin over framboise or juice. Let soften for about 3 minutes, then swirl over very low heat just until the gelatin is dissolved. Let cool to room temperature.

3. In a medium bowl, whip cream to firm peaks. Whisk in the gelatin mixture. With a rubber spatula, fold this cream mixture into the cooled meringue, then fold in 1½ cups of the raspberries. Cover and refrigerate until firm and well chilled, about 1 hour.

TO ASSEMBLE CAKE:

Unroll the cooled cake, remove the paper and spread with the raspberry filling. Gently roll it up again and place it on a serving platter, seam-side down. Refrigerate for at least 1 hour or overnight. Dust lightly with additional cocoa just before serving. Serve with Raspberry-Chocolate Sauce, if you like, and garnish with the remaining ½ cup raspberries.

Serves 12.

135 calories per serving: 3 grams protein, 3 grams fat (2 grams saturated fat), 21 grams carbohydrate, 1 gram alcohol; 108 mg sodium; 43 mg cholesterol.

FILLING

2	large egg whites
½	cup sugar
¼	teaspoon cream of tartar
1¼	teaspoons unflavored gelatin
3	tablespoons eau-de-vie de framboise *or* cran-raspberry juice
⅓	cup chilled whipping cream
2	cups fresh raspberries

♦ **INGREDIENT NOTE**

Eau-de-vie de framboise is a clear alcohol made from raspberries. It has an intense fruity aroma and flavor.

Chocolate-Cherry Bars

CHOCOLATE-CHERRY BARS

Dramatically dark in color, these chewy bars are studded with dried tart cherries.

2 large eggs

1 large egg white

¾ cup sugar

2 teaspoons pure vanilla extract

¼ teaspoon salt

2 cups chocolate wafer crumbs (about 40 wafers)

1 cup chopped dried tart cherries

¼ cup chopped walnuts

1. Preheat oven to 325°F. Lightly oil an 8-by-12-inch or 7-by-11-inch baking pan or coat it with nonstick cooking spray; set aside.

2. In a large bowl, beat together eggs, egg white, sugar, vanilla and salt with an electric mixer on high speed until the eggs are thick and pale, about 2 minutes. With a rubber spatula, gently fold in chocolate wafer crumbs and cherries just until combined. Transfer the batter to the prepared baking pan; smooth the top. Sprinkle with walnuts. Bake for 30 to 35 minutes, or until a skewer inserted in the center comes out clean.

3. Let cool in the baking pan on a wire rack. Cut into bars. (*Store at room temperature in an airtight container.*)

Makes 15 bars.

150 calories per bar: 3 grams protein, 4 grams fat (0 grams saturated fat), 27 grams carbohydrate; 157 mg sodium; 31 mg cholesterol.

CHOCOLATE CHEESECAKE

The chocolate flavor in this rich and glossy cheesecake is deepened by the addition of coffee.

TO MAKE CRUST:

Preheat oven to 325°F. Lightly oil a 9-inch springform pan or coat it with nonstick cooking spray. Place chocolate wafers, Grape-Nuts, cocoa and sugar in a food processor; pulse until you have fine crumbs. Add oil and 3 tablespoons water; process until the crumbs are moistened. Press the crumb mixture into the bottom and about 1½ inches up the sides of the prepared pan. Set aside.

TO MAKE FILLING:

1. Melt chocolate in the top of a double boiler over hot, not boiling, water or in a microwave oven at medium (50 percent) power. Let cool slightly. Dissolve instant coffee in 1 tablespoon boiling water and set aside.

2. Place cottage cheese in a strainer lined with a double thickness of cheesecloth. Gather up the cheesecloth and squeeze out the moisture from the cottage cheese. Put the pressed cottage-cheese solids in a food processor and blend until completely smooth, about 2 minutes. Add cream cheese, sugar, egg, egg whites, sour cream, cocoa, cornstarch, salt, vanilla, the melted chocolate and the dissolved coffee; process until smooth. Pour into the crumb-lined pan.

3. Bake for about 1 hour, or until firm around the edge but still shiny and slightly soft in the center. Run a knife around the pan to loosen the edges. Let cool in the pan on a wire rack. Cover and refrigerate until well chilled, at least 8 hours or for up to 2 days. Remove the outer ring of the pan. To facilitate cutting, dip a sharp knife in hot water and wipe dry before cutting each slice.

Serves 16.

280 calories per serving: 12 grams protein, 10 grams fat (4 grams saturated fat), 36 grams carbohydrate; 424 mg sodium; 33 mg cholesterol.

CRUST

4	ounces chocolate wafers (18 wafers)
1	cup Grape-Nuts cereal
2	tablespoons unsweetened cocoa powder, preferably Dutch-process
2	tablespoons sugar
3	tablespoons canola oil

FILLING

2	ounces semisweet chocolate
2	tablespoons instant coffee powder
32	ounces nonfat cottage cheese (4 cups)
8	ounces reduced-fat cream cheese, at room temperature
1½	cups sugar
1	large egg
2	large egg whites
1	cup reduced-fat sour cream
¾	cup unsweetened cocoa powder, preferably Dutch-process
2	tablespoons cornstarch
⅛	teaspoon salt
1	teaspoon pure vanilla extract

◆**INGREDIENT NOTE**

Commercial chocolate wafers are very low in fat yet pack a rich chocolate flavor. They work well for this crumb crust and for the Chocolate-Cherry Bars on page 100.

CHOCOLATE ANGEL FOOD CAKE

Serve this cake with frozen yogurt and fresh fruit.

¼ cup unsweetened cocoa powder (*not* Dutch-process)

¼ cup hot, strong coffee

1¼ cups sugar

¾ cup sifted cake flour

¼ teaspoon salt

12 large egg whites, at room temperature

1 teaspoon cream of tartar

1. Preheat oven to 350°F. Have ready a 10-inch tube pan and a long-necked bottle or funnel. In a medium bowl, dissolve cocoa in coffee; set aside and let cool to room temperature. In another bowl, combine ½ cup of the sugar, flour and salt; set aside.

2. Place egg whites in a large mixing bowl. Using an electric mixer, beat the egg whites until frothy. Add cream of tartar and continue beating until soft peaks form. Gradually add the remaining ¾ cup sugar and beat just until stiff peaks form. Do not overbeat.

3. Sift the dry ingredients over the beaten egg whites in 3 parts, folding in gently after each sifting. Stir approximately 1 cup of the egg-white mixture into the coffee mixture. Fold it back into the egg-white mixture until thoroughly combined. Pour the batter into the ungreased tube pan. Smooth the top and run a small knife or spatula through the batter to remove any air pockets.

4. Bake for 50 to 60 minutes, or until a skewer comes out clean and the top springs back when touched lightly. Invert the pan over the bottle and let cool completely. Turn the cake right-side up and, with a knife, loosen the edges. Invert the cake onto a serving platter.

Serves 16.

91 calories per serving: 3 grams protein, 0 grams fat, 19 grams carbohydrate; 74 mg sodium; 0 mg cholesterol.

◆**ANGEL FOOD SUCCESS**
Avoid any traces of yolk in the egg whites, which will keep them from whipping. Also, grease in the tube pan will interfere with the rising of the batter.

CHOCOLATE PUDDING CAKE WITH COFFEE SAUCE

As this fudgy pudding cake bakes, the sauce forms in the bottom of the dish beneath a tender blanket of chocolate cake.

1. Preheat oven to 375°F. Coat six 10-ounce custard cups or ramekins lightly with oil or nonstick cooking spray and set them on a baking sheet.

2. Spread nuts in a pie pan and toast in the oven for 5 to 10 minutes, or until fragrant. In a large bowl, stir together flour, sugar, cocoa, baking powder and salt. In a measuring cup, stir together milk, egg, oil and vanilla. Add to the dry ingredients and stir just until combined. Divide the batter among the prepared custard cups or ramekins. In a measuring cup, stir together hot coffee and brown sugar. Pour about one-sixth of the coffee mixture over each dessert. Sprinkle with the reserved toasted nuts.

3. Bake for 15 to 20 minutes, or until the tops spring back when touched lightly. Cool for 5 minutes. Sprinkle with confectioners' sugar and serve hot or warm.

Serves 6.

305 calories per serving: 5 grams protein, 7 grams fat (1 gram saturated fat), 55 grams carbohydrate; 318 mg sodium; 36 mg cholesterol.

2 tablespoons chopped walnuts *or* pecans

1 cup all-purpose white flour

⅓ cup sugar

¾ cup unsweetened cocoa powder, preferably Dutch-process, sifted

2 teaspoons baking powder

½ teaspoon salt

½ cup skim milk

1 large egg, lightly beaten

2 tablespoons walnut oil *or* canola oil

2 teaspoons pure vanilla extract

1⅓ cups hot brewed coffee *or* 1½ tablespoons instant coffee granules dissolved in 1⅓ cups boiling water

¾ cup light *or* dark brown sugar

Confectioners' sugar for dusting

◆**MAXIMIZING THE FLAVOR OF NUTS**
A small amount of toasted walnuts coupled with walnut oil gives a great deal of flavor to this dessert.

Chocolate-Dipped Apricots

CHOCOLATE-DIPPED APRICOTS

Tart apricots are a vibrant counterpoint to dark chocolate in these moist jewels, perfect with after-dinner coffee.

⅓ cup sugar

2 strips lemon zest

1 cinnamon stick

24 dried apricots
    (about ¼ pound)

2 ounces bittersweet (*not* unsweetened) chocolate, melted

1 tablespoon chopped peeled pistachios

1. Line a baking sheet with wax paper and place a wire rack on top; set aside. In a small saucepan, combine sugar, lemon zest, cinnamon stick and 1 cup water; bring to a boil, stirring to dissolve the sugar. Reduce the heat to medium and simmer for 3 minutes. Add apricots and simmer gently just until tender, 6 to 8 minutes. With a slotted spoon, transfer the apricots to the rack. Let cool completely.

2. Dip half of a poached apricot in melted chocolate, letting the excess drip off. Sprinkle some chopped pistachios over the chocolate half and return the apricot to the rack. Repeat with the remaining apricots. (You will have some melted chocolate left over.) Refrigerate until the chocolate has set, about 20 minutes. (*The candies may be stored in an airtight container, with wax paper between each layer, in the refrigerator for up to 1 week.*)

Makes 24 pieces.

30 calories per candy: 0 grams protein, 1 gram fat (0 grams saturated fat), 6 grams carbohydrate; 1 mg sodium; 0 mg cholesterol.

♦**MELTING CHOCOLATE**

Coarsely chop chocolate and melt in a small metal bowl set over a pan of barely simmering water or in a small glass bowl in the microwave on medium-low power (30%) for about 2 minutes, stirring once or twice.

CHOCOLATE-BANANA LUNCHBOX CAKE

To ensure that this cake lasts long enough for at least one week's worth of lunches, wrap individual pieces in plastic wrap and store them in the freezer.

1. Preheat oven to 400°F. Lightly oil an 8-by-12-inch or 7-by-11-inch baking pan or coat it with nonstick cooking spray.

2. In a mixing bowl, whisk flour, cocoa, baking soda and salt. In another bowl, whisk mashed banana, buttermilk, brown sugar, corn syrup, oil and vanilla. Make a well in the center of the dry ingredients and add the banana mixture; mix with a wooden spoon or rubber spatula just until the dry ingredients are moistened.

3. Transfer the batter to the prepared baking pan, smoothing the top. Sprinkle chocolate chips and nuts over the top. Bake for about 20 minutes, or until a skewer inserted in the center comes out clean. Let cool in the pan, dust with confectioners' sugar and cut into squares.

Serves 12.

220 calories per serving: 3 grams protein, 6 grams fat (1 gram saturated fat), 40 grams carbohydrate; 182 mg sodium; 1 mg cholesterol.

2 cups sifted cake flour

2 tablespoons unsweetened cocoa powder (*not* Dutch-process)

1 teaspoon baking soda

½ teaspoon salt

¾ cup mashed very ripe banana (2 small bananas)

¾ cup buttermilk

⅔ cup packed light *or* dark brown sugar

¼ cup dark corn syrup

3 tablespoons canola oil

1 tablespoon pure vanilla extract

⅓ cup chocolate chips

2 tablespoons chopped walnuts *or* pecans

Confectioners' sugar for dusting

◆ **STRETCHING HIGH-FAT INGREDIENTS**

Small amounts of high-fat goodies like nuts or chocolate chips have a lot more impact when sprinkled on top of a dessert, rather than mixed into it.

FUDGE CAKE IN A MERINGUE CHEMISE

A moist, fudgy chocolate cake enclosed in a layer of crunchy pecan meringue, this is worthy of any celebration.

CHOCOLATE GLAZE

⅓	cup sugar
3	tablespoons unsweetened cocoa powder, preferably Dutch-process
½	cup evaporated skim milk
1½	ounces bittersweet (*not* unsweetened) chocolate, coarsely chopped
½	teaspoon pure vanilla extract

CHOCOLATE CAKE & MERINGUE

¾	cup chopped pitted dates
½	cup pecan halves
1	ounce unsweetened chocolate
1½	cups cake flour (unsifted)
⅓	cup unsweetened cocoa powder, preferably Dutch-process
1	teaspoon baking powder
½	teaspoon baking soda
½	teaspoon salt
1	large egg, lightly beaten
1¾	cups sugar
¼	cup canola oil
1	teaspoon pure vanilla extract
1	teaspoon instant coffee granules
1	cup buttermilk
3	large egg whites

TO MAKE CHOCOLATE GLAZE:

In a small heavy saucepan, combine sugar and cocoa. Add ¼ cup of the evaporated skim milk and whisk until you have a smooth paste. Add the remaining evaporated skim milk, place over medium heat and bring to a boil, whisking constantly. Cook at a gentle boil, stirring almost constantly, for 2 minutes. Remove from the heat and add bittersweet chocolate; stir until melted. Stir in vanilla. Pour into a bowl, cover and refrigerate until chilled and thickened, about 2 hours.

TO MAKE CHOCOLATE CAKE & MERINGUE:

1. Preheat oven to 325°F. Lightly oil a 9- or 10-inch tube pan (with flat bottom and unfluted sides) or coat it with nonstick cooking spray. Line the bottom with parchment or wax paper; set aside.

2. In a small saucepan, combine dates with ⅓ cup water; bring to a simmer over medium heat. Cook, stirring frequently, until the dates have softened and absorbed most of the liquid, 2 to 3 minutes. Transfer to a mixing bowl and let cool completely.

3. Spread pecans in a shallow baking pan and bake for 5 to 7 minutes, or until fragrant. Select 16 pecan halves for garnish; set aside. Once the remaining pecans are cool, finely chop them. Grate unsweetened chocolate; set aside.

4. Sift flour, cocoa, baking powder, baking soda and salt into a bowl; set aside.

5. When the dates have cooled, add egg, 1 cup sugar, oil, vanilla and coffee granules; beat with an electric mixer for 1 minute. With a rubber spatula, alternately fold the reserved flour mixture and buttermilk into the date/egg mixture, making 3 additions of dry ingredients and 2 additions of buttermilk. Set the cake batter aside.

6. In a clean mixing bowl, with clean beaters, beat egg whites with an electric mixer until soft peaks form. Gradually add the remaining ¾ cup sugar, beating until stiff, glossy peaks form. With a rubber spatula, fold in the reserved grated chocolate and chopped pecans. Spread the meringue on the bottom of the prepared pan and three-quarters of the way up the sides, as though lining it. Pour the reserved cake batter into the pan. (It should be surrounded on all sides by meringue.)

Fudge Cake in a Meringue Chemise

7. Bake for 60 to 65 minutes, or until the top of the cake springs back when touched lightly and the meringue is crisp. If necessary, trim away any meringue that protrudes above the surface of the cake. Let the cake cool in the pan on a rack for 30 minutes. Carefully separate the meringue from the pan with a metal spatula, then turn the cake out onto a serving plate. Peel off parchment or wax paper and let cool completely.

TO GLAZE CAKE:

Carefully pour the chilled chocolate glaze over the cake, spreading gently so that it drips down the sides. Arrange the reserved pecan halves around the top of the cake.

Serves 16.

210 calories per serving: 3 grams protein, 8 grams fat (1 gram saturated fat), 36 grams carbohydrate; 148 mg sodium; 14 mg cholesterol.

◆**FAT-CUTTING TIP**

Dates are the magic ingredient in this low-fat cake. Using the fruit enabled us to cut the oil in the recipe to a mere ¼ cup.

BROWNIES

The combination of full-flavored Dutch-process cocoa, canola oil and moist brown sugar produces a classic fudgy brownie that is low in fat and free of saturated fat.

1	cup sifted cake flour
½	cup Dutch-process cocoa powder
½	teaspoon salt
1½	cups packed light brown sugar
¼	cup canola oil
¼	cup buttermilk
1	large egg
2	large egg whites
2	teaspoons pure vanilla extract

1. Preheat oven to 350°F. Lightly oil an 8-by-12-inch or 7-by-11-inch baking pan or coat it with nonstick cooking spray. Dust with a little flour, tapping out the excess, and set aside.

2. In a small bowl, whisk together flour, cocoa and salt. In a large bowl, beat together brown sugar, oil, buttermilk, egg, egg whites and vanilla with an electric mixer on high speed until smooth, making sure no lumps of brown sugar remain. Add the dry ingredients and beat on low speed just until blended.

3. Transfer the batter to the prepared baking pan. Bake for 25 to 30 minutes, or just until a skewer inserted in the center comes out clean. Let cool in the baking pan on a rack. Cut into bars. (*Store at room temperature in an airtight container.*)

Makes 15 bars.

155 calories per brownie: 2 grams protein, 4 grams fat (0 grams saturated fat), 29 grams carbohydrate; 95 mg sodium; 14 mg cholesterol.

◆**SUBSTITUTION**

If you don't have Dutch-process cocoa, you can use American-style (nonalkalized) cocoa and add ½ teaspoon of baking soda to the dry ingredients to neutralize the slightly sour taste from the cocoa.

THE WELL-STOCKED COOKIE JAR

Grandma's cookie jar is probably a collector's item today. Remember the wonderful cookies she used to make? First she creamed two sticks of butter and a cup of sugar... Ah, the good old days.

Our initial attempts at creating fat-free versions of Grandma's cookies produced gummy results. We put a little of the fat back in, however, and classics like Peanut Butter Cookies and Brown Sugar Crackles are the chewy, crisp proof of our success. Another tactic was to sample the international cookie repertoire,  where we discovered recipes that are naturally low in fat, such as German lebkuchen and Italian biscotti. Here are some new treats for the old precious cookie jar on your kitchen shelf.

SICILIAN FIG COOKIES

A crisp pastry surrounds the moist filling made of dried figs, apricots, dates and raisins.
These are delicious without the icing as well. A perfect Christmas cookie.

COOKIE DOUGH

2½   cups all-purpose white flour

⅓   cup sugar

1¼   teaspoons baking powder

½   teaspoon salt

3   tablespoons butter, cut into small pieces

1   large egg

1   large egg white

¼   cup low-fat milk

2½   tablespoons canola oil

1   teaspoon pure vanilla extract

¼   teaspoon pure almond extract

FILLING

¼   cup slivered almonds

¼   teaspoon aniseed

2   cups dried figs, stems removed

1   cup dried apricots

½   cup chopped dates

½   cup golden raisins

⅓   cup sugar

1½   teaspoons grated lemon zest

1½   teaspoons ground cinnamon

⅛   teaspoon freshly ground black pepper

⅓   cup Marsala *or* fresh orange juice

TO MAKE COOKIE DOUGH:

Combine flour, sugar, baking powder and salt in the food processor. Add butter and pulse until the butter is in very small pieces, about 10 seconds. In a large glass measuring cup, whisk together egg, egg white, milk, oil, vanilla and almond extracts; with the food processor running, pour in the liquid and mix just until a smooth dough forms. Scrape the dough onto wax paper or plastic wrap and flatten into a 1-inch-thick disk. Wrap and refrigerate overnight or for up to 2 days.

TO MAKE FILLING:

1. Preheat oven to 350°F. Spread almonds on a baking sheet or in a pie pan. Toast for 3 minutes; add aniseed and continue to toast until the nuts are pale gold and the aniseed is fragrant, about 3 minutes longer. Set aside to cool.

2. In the food processor, combine figs, apricots, dates, raisins, sugar, lemon zest, cinnamon, pepper and the toasted almonds and aniseed. Pulse until the fruits and nuts are finely chopped. With the machine running, pour Marsala or orange juice through the feed tube and process until just blended. (*Use immediately, or cover with plastic wrap and refrigerate for up to 2 days. Return the filling to room temperature before using.*)

TO BAKE COOKIES:

1. Preheat oven to 350°F. Lightly oil 2 large baking sheets or coat them with nonstick cooking spray. Divide the dough into 6 equal pieces. Working with one piece at a time (keeping the remaining pieces refrigerated), roll out on a lightly floured surface into a 4-by-12-inch rectangle. (Don't worry if the edges are ragged.) Measure a scant ½ cup of the filling and use your hands to spread it in a strip down the center of the dough.

2. Use a wide spatula or pastry scraper to lift the sides of the dough over the filling to form a roll. Use your fingers to press down the seam, which may be a bit ragged and uneven. With a sharp knife, slice the roll on the diagonal into 1-inch-long cookies. Set the cookies on a prepared baking sheet, spacing them about 1 inch apart. Repeat these steps with the remaining dough and filling.

3. Bake the cookies, one sheet at a time, for 15 to 18 minutes, or until the bottoms are pale golden and the tops are lightly colored. Transfer the cookies to a wire rack to cool.

TO MAKE ICING:

In a small bowl, whisk together confectioners' sugar, milk, vanilla and almond extracts until smooth. Place the cookies close together on wax paper. Drizzle the tops of the cookies liberally with icing. (*Store the cookies in an airtight container for up to 4 days.*)

Makes about 5 dozen cookies.

80 calories per cookie: 1 gram protein, 2 grams fat (0 grams saturated fat), 16 grams carbohydrate; 26 mg sodium; 5 mg cholesterol.

ICING

1¼ cups confectioners' sugar

2 tablespoons low-fat milk, plus more as needed

¼ teaspoon pure vanilla extract

¼ teaspoon pure almond extract

PINE NUT COOKIES

These cookies should be made on a dry day so they turn out crisp.

1. Preheat oven to 250°F. Line 2 baking sheets with parchment paper and set aside.

2. In a mixing bowl, beat egg whites and salt with an electric mixer on low speed until foamy; raise the speed to high. When the whites begin to form soft peaks, gradually add sugar, beating until the whites are shiny with no traces of grittiness and form stiff peaks. With a rubber spatula, fold in pine nuts and lemon zest. Drop tablespoonfuls of the batter, about 1 inch apart, on the prepared baking sheets.

3. Bake for 40 minutes, switching the positions of the baking sheets midway; turn off the oven and leave the cookies in the closed oven to dry for 3 more hours. Peel the cookies off the parchment paper. (*Store in an airtight container at room temperature for up to 1 week.*)

Makes 3 dozen cookies.

20 calories per cookie: 1 gram protein, 1 gram fat (0 grams saturated fat), 3 grams carbohydrate; 5 mg sodium; 0 mg cholesterol.

3 large egg whites, at room temperature

Pinch of salt

½ cup sugar

½ cup pine nuts

2 teaspoons grated lemon zest

◆**STORAGE TIP**

Pine nuts should be stored in the freezer.

Brown Sugar Crackles

BROWN SUGAR CRACKLES

These sweet sugar cookies have an appealing crazed top and a chewy middle.

1. Preheat oven to 350°F. Lightly oil 3 baking sheets or coat them with nonstick cooking spray and set aside.

2. In a small bowl, stir together white and whole-wheat flours, baking powder, baking soda and salt. In a mixing bowl, beat together brown sugar, butter, oil, eggs and vanilla with an electric mixer on high speed until smooth, making sure no lumps of brown sugar remain, about 1 minute. Stir in the dry ingredients until completely blended. (The dough will be stiff.)

3. Divide the dough in half and press each half into a flat disk. On a lightly floured surface, roll out one of the disks to a ¼-inch thickness. Cut out cookies with a 2-inch round cookie cutter, placing the cookies 1 inch apart on the prepared baking sheets. Repeat with the remaining dough. Press the scraps together and cut out additional cookies.

4. Bake the cookies, one sheet at a time, for 8 to 10 minutes, or until they are puffed in the middle and browned around the edges. Let stand for about 2 minutes on the baking sheets, then remove to a wire rack to cool completely. (*Store the cookies in an airtight container for up to 3 days.*)

Makes about 4 dozen cookies.

80 calories per cookie: 1 gram protein, 2 grams fat (1 gram saturated fat), 14 grams carbohydrate; 84 mg sodium; 11 mg cholesterol.

2 cups all-purpose white flour

⅔ cup whole-wheat flour

1 teaspoon baking powder

1 teaspoon baking soda

1 teaspoon salt

2 cups packed light brown sugar

¼ cup butter, softened

¼ cup canola oil

2 large eggs

2 teaspoons pure vanilla extract

PEPPERED LEBKUCHEN

These Christmas cookies are great with a cup of coffee at any time of the year.
Lebkuchen get even better after a few days as they mellow to a wonderful deep flavor.

COOKIE DOUGH

- 2 cups all-purpose white flour
- 1 teaspoon freshly grated nutmeg
- 1 teaspoon ground cinnamon
- 1 teaspoon ground allspice
- ½ teaspoon ground cloves
- ½ teaspoon ground ginger
- ¼ teaspoon ground mace
- ¼ teaspoon baking soda
- ¼ teaspoon salt
- ¼ teaspoon freshly ground black pepper
- ½ cup honey
- ½ cup packed dark brown sugar
- 1 large egg
- 1½ teaspoons grated lemon zest
- 1½ teaspoons grated orange zest

GLAZE

- ¼ cup confectioners' sugar
- 2 teaspoons fresh lemon juice
- 1 teaspoon fresh orange juice
- ½ teaspoon grated lemon zest
- ½ teaspoon grated orange zest

TO MAKE COOKIE DOUGH:

In a mixing bowl, whisk together flour, nutmeg, cinnamon, allspice, cloves, ginger, mace, baking soda, salt and pepper until thoroughly combined. In another, larger mixing bowl, blend honey, brown sugar, egg and lemon and orange zests. Add the dry ingredients and stir to make a smooth, somewhat soft and sticky dough. Transfer the dough onto wax paper or plastic wrap and shape into a flat, ½-inch-thick disk. Wrap and refrigerate at least 4 hours or overnight.

TO MAKE GLAZE:

In a small bowl, whisk together confectioners' sugar, citrus juices and zests until smooth. Cover and set aside.

TO BAKE COOKIES:

1. Preheat oven to 350°F. Lightly oil 2 large baking sheets or coat them with nonstick cooking spray. Working with half of the dough at a time, roll it out on a lightly floured surface into a large rectangle slightly less than ¼ inch thick. With a pastry wheel or pizza cutter, trim the edges and cut into 1¼-by-2-inch rectangles. Transfer the cookies to the prepared baking sheets, spacing them about 1 inch apart.

2. Bake the cookies, one sheet at a time, for 8 to 10 minutes, or until the edges are lightly colored and the cookies are firm. Immediately transfer to a wire rack. Brush the tops of the warm cookies with the reserved glaze. Let stand until the glaze sets, about 1 hour. (*Store the lebkuchen in an airtight container for up to 3 weeks.*)

Makes about 4 dozen cookies.

45 calories per cookie: 1 gram protein, 0 grams fat, 10 grams carbohydrate; 18 mg sodium; 4 mg cholesterol.

MORAVIAN SPICE COOKIES

The Moravian Settlement in Old Salem, North Carolina, is famous for its tins of crisp, spicy wafers very similar to these.

1. In a small saucepan, melt butter over low heat. Cook, swirling the pan, until the butter turns a nutty brown, about 1 minute. Add molasses, brown sugar and oil, stirring to melt the sugar. Transfer to a mixing bowl and let cool for 5 minutes.

2. Add cinnamon, ginger, cloves, allspice and baking soda to the bowl and beat in with an electric mixer on medium speed. With the mixer on low speed, add flour, ½ cup at a time, beating just until incorporated.

3. Turn the dough out onto a large sheet of plastic wrap; flatten it into a disk and wrap it up. Let the dough rest at room temperature for 1 to 2 hours before rolling. (*Alternatively, the dough can be made up to 3 days in advance and stored in the refrigerator. Bring to room temperature before rolling.*)

4. Preheat oven to 350°F. Lightly oil 2 baking sheets or coat them with nonstick cooking spray. Divide the dough in half and rewrap the unused portion. On a floured surface, roll the dough out as thin as possible, less than ¹⁄₁₆ inch. Cut out cookies with a small (2-inch) cutter and place them about ¼ inch apart on the prepared baking sheets. Bake, one sheet at a time, for 8 to 10 minutes, or until the cookies are crisp and just beginning to brown on the edges. Transfer to a wire rack to cool. Repeat with the remaining dough. (*Store the cookies in an airtight container for up to 2 weeks.*)

Makes about 6 dozen cookies.

30 calories per cookie: 0 grams protein, 1 gram fat (0 grams saturated fat), 5 grams carbohydrate; 6 mg sodium; 1 mg cholesterol.

2	tablespoons butter
½	cup molasses
¼	cup dark brown sugar
2	tablespoons canola oil
1	teaspoon ground cinnamon
½	teaspoon ground ginger
½	teaspoon ground cloves
½	teaspoon ground allspice
½	teaspoon baking soda
2	cups all-purpose white flour

FILLED OATMEAL-DATE COOKIES

These sturdy cookies are just right for the lunchbox.

FILLING

1½ cups chopped pitted dates

⅓ cup packed light brown sugar

2 teaspoons fresh lemon juice

1 teaspoon grated lemon zest

DOUGH

¼ cup pecans *or* walnuts

1½ cups packed light brown sugar

1 large egg

2 large egg whites

¼ cup canola oil

¼ cup apple butter

2 teaspoons pure vanilla extract

2 cups all-purpose white flour

1 teaspoon baking soda

1 teaspoon ground cinnamon

1 teaspoon salt

½ teaspoon baking powder

2 cups rolled oats

TO MAKE FILLING:

In a small saucepan, combine dates, brown sugar, lemon juice, lemon zest and ⅓ cup water. Bring to a simmer over medium heat. Cook, stirring, until thickened, about 30 seconds. Set aside to cool.

TO MAKE DOUGH:

1. Place rack in upper third of oven; preheat to 350°F. Lightly oil 3 baking sheets or coat them with nonstick cooking spray; set aside. Spread nuts in a pie pan and toast in the oven until fragrant and lightly browned, about 5 minutes. Let cool briefly, then finely chop.

2. In a large mixing bowl, combine brown sugar, egg, egg whites, oil, apple butter and vanilla. Beat with an electric mixer until smooth and pale in color, about 2 minutes. Sift flour, baking soda, cinnamon, salt and baking powder into the mixing bowl. Add rolled oats and stir until well combined.

3. Drop the dough by heaping teaspoonfuls onto the prepared baking sheets, spacing cookies about 1½ inches apart. With the back of a teaspoon, dipped in water to prevent sticking, make a depression in the center of each mound. Fill with a scant teaspoon of the reserved date filling. Top with another heaping teaspoon of dough, spreading it to roughly cover the filling. Sprinkle each cookie with a scant ¼ teaspoon of the toasted nuts. Bake, 1 sheet at a time, for 12 to 15 minutes, or until lightly browned on top. Transfer the cookies to wire racks to cool. (*If keeping for longer than 1 day, freeze in an airtight container with wax paper between the layers.*)

Makes about 3 dozen cookies.

130 calories per cookie: 2 grams protein, 3 grams fat (0 grams saturated fat), 25 grams carbohydrate; 95 mg sodium; 6 mg cholesterol.

◆**STORAGE NOTE**
Store reduced-fat cookies in the freezer to help keep their flavor fresh.

RUGELACH

Expect some of the filling to ooze out during baking, but don't worry—there will still be plenty inside the cookie.

TO MAKE DOUGH:

Place cottage cheese on a double thickness of cheesecloth. Gather up the corners of the cheesecloth and firmly squeeze out all the moisture; you should end up with 1 cup of cottage cheese. In a mixing bowl, beat the cottage cheese, cream cheese, sugar, oil, butter and vanilla with an electric mixer until light and fluffy. Mix together flour and salt and add to the cheese mixture; stir with a wooden spoon until just blended. Wrap the dough in wax paper, then in plastic wrap, and chill for at least 2 hours or preferably overnight.

TO MAKE FILLING:

1. Set oven rack in upper third of oven; preheat to 350°F. Spread walnuts on a pie pan and toast in the oven 5 to 10 minutes, until fragrant and lightly browned. Let cool briefly, then chop. Prepare 2 baking sheets by coating with nonstick cooking spray or lining with parchment paper.

2. In a small bowl, stir together brown sugar, Grape-Nuts, cinnamon and the chopped walnuts. Cover and set aside.

TO FORM AND BAKE RUGELACH:

1. Divide the dough into four equal parts. On a lightly floured surface, roll each portion into a 10-inch-diameter circle. (Keep the remaining dough chilled until ready to use.) Sprinkle with one-fourth of the brown-sugar mixture and 2 tablespoons currants, pressing slightly so that the filling adheres. Cut the circle into 8 wedges. Beginning at the widest end, roll up each wedge and curve into a crescent. Place on a prepared baking sheet. Repeat with the remaining dough.

2. Bake for 20 to 25 minutes, or until tops are light brown. Immediately transfer to a wire rack and let cool. (*Store in an airtight container, with wax paper between the layers, for up to 4 days.*)

Makes 32 rugelach.

100 calories per rugelach: 3 grams protein, 3 grams fat (1 gram saturated fat), 17 grams carbohydrate; 66 mg sodium; 4 mg cholesterol.

DOUGH

- 2 cups nonfat cottage cheese
- 4 ounces reduced-fat cream cheese (½ cup)
- ½ cup sugar
- 2 tablespoons canola oil
- 2 tablespoons butter, softened
- 1 teaspoon pure vanilla extract
- 3 cups sifted cake flour
- ½ teaspoon salt

FILLING

- 2 tablespoons walnuts
- ½ cup packed light brown sugar
- 2 tablespoons Grape-Nuts cereal
- 1 teaspoon ground cinnamon
- ½ cup currants

◆**LOW-FAT BAKING**
Grape-Nuts cereal has a crunch and flavor similar to real nuts, so mixing the two in fillings and crusts is a good fat-reducing trick.

HAZELNUT-ANISE BISCOTTI

Crunchy and dry, these biscotti are perfect for dipping in a glass of sweet wine, coffee or tea.

1	cup hazelnuts (filberts)
2¼	cups all-purpose white flour
4	teaspoons aniseed
1	teaspoon baking powder
½	teaspoon salt
3	large eggs
1	cup sugar
1	teaspoon pure vanilla extract

1. Preheat oven to 325°F. Lightly oil a baking sheet or coat it with nonstick cooking spray and set aside. Spread hazelnuts in a pie pan and bake for 8 to 12 minutes, or until lightly toasted. If the hazelnuts have skins, place them in a clean kitchen towel, fold the towel over and rub off the skins. Let cool.

2. In a mixing bowl, stir together flour, aniseed, baking powder and salt. In another mixing bowl, beat eggs, sugar and vanilla with an electric mixer on high speed until thick and pale, about 3 minutes. With a wooden spoon, stir in the dry ingredients, followed by the hazelnuts (the dough will be very soft and sticky).

3. With two rubber spatulas, form the dough into three 10-inch-long logs on the prepared baking sheet. Smooth the logs with a spatula or moistened hands.

4. Bake for 30 minutes, or until the logs are lightly browned and spring back when lightly pressed in the center. Carefully transfer the logs to a cutting board; slice them crosswise into ½-inch-thick slices. Stand the slices upright on a baking sheet, ½ inch apart. Return the biscotti to the oven to bake for 10 to 15 minutes longer, or until lightly colored and crisp. Transfer the biscotti to a wire rack to cool. (*Store the biscotti in an airtight container for up to 1 month.*)

Makes about 4 dozen biscotti.

60 calories per biscotto: 1 gram protein, 2 grams fat (0 grams saturated fat), 9 grams carbohydrate; 33 mg sodium; 13 mg cholesterol.

♦**INGREDIENT NOTE**

Hazelnuts, also called filberts, are rich in monounsaturated fats. The shelled nuts quickly go rancid at room temperature; store them in the refrigerator or freezer.

Hazelnut-Anise Biscotti (*left*) & Poppy Seed-Orange Biscotti (*page 120*)

POPPY SEED-ORANGE BISCOTTI

The flavor of biscotti actually improves after a few days in an airtight tin, and they keep well for a month or longer. They are wonderful to have on hand to serve with midafternoon tea or postdinner coffee. (Photograph on page 119.)

2 cups all-purpose white flour

1 cup sugar

¼ cup poppy seeds

1 teaspoon baking powder

½ teaspoon baking soda

¼ teaspoon salt

2 large eggs

2 large egg whites

3 tablespoons grated orange zest

1 tablespoon frozen orange-juice concentrate, thawed

1. Preheat oven to 325°F. Lightly oil a baking sheet or coat it with nonstick cooking spray; set aside.

2. In a mixing bowl, combine flour, sugar, poppy seeds, baking powder, baking soda and salt. In another mixing bowl, whisk together eggs, egg whites, orange zest and orange-juice concentrate. Add to the dry ingredients and mix well. The dough will be very soft and sticky.

3. Working on a very well-floured surface, shape the dough into 2 logs, each about 14 inches long and 1½ inches thick. Place the logs on the prepared baking sheet and bake for 20 to 25 minutes, or until firm to the touch. Transfer the logs to a cutting board to cool. Reduce the oven temperature to 300°F.

4. Slice the logs diagonally into ½-inch-thick slices. Stand the slices upright on the baking sheet, ½ inch apart, and bake for 40 minutes. Transfer biscotti to a wire rack to cool. *(Store in an airtight container for up to 1 month.)*

Makes about 4 dozen biscotti.

40 calories per biscotto: 1 gram protein, 1 gram fat (0 grams saturated fat), 8 grams carbohydrate; 32 mg sodium; 9 mg cholesterol.

LEMON THINS

Light and citrusy, this is the perfect cookie to pair with sorbets or summery fruit compotes.

1. Preheat oven to 350°F. Lightly oil 2 baking sheets or coat them with nonstick cooking spray. In a mixing bowl, whisk together flour, cornstarch, baking powder and salt; set aside.

2. In a mixing bowl, cream ½ cup of the sugar, butter and oil with an electric mixer on medium speed until fluffy. Add egg white, lemon zest and vanilla; beat until smooth. Beat in lemon juice. Add the dry ingredients and fold in with a rubber spatula just until combined.

3. Drop the dough by teaspoonfuls, 2 inches apart, onto the prepared baking sheets. Place the remaining ¼ cup sugar in a saucer. Spray the bottom of a wide-bottomed glass with nonstick cooking spray and dip it in the sugar. Flatten the dough with the glass into 2½-inch circles, dipping the glass in the sugar each time.

4. Bake for 8 to 10 minutes, or until the cookies are just starting to brown around the edges. Transfer the cookies to a flat surface (not a rack) to crisp. (*Store in an airtight container for up to 3 days.*)

Makes 2½ dozen cookies.

60 calories per cookie: 1 gram protein, 2 grams fat (1 gram saturated fat), 10 grams carbohydrate; 44 mg sodium; 9 mg cholesterol.

1¼	cups all-purpose white flour
⅓	cup cornstarch
1½	teaspoons baking powder
¼	teaspoon salt
¾	cup sugar
2	tablespoons butter, softened
2	tablespoons canola oil
1	large egg white
1½	teaspoons grated lemon zest
1	teaspoon pure vanilla extract
3	tablespoons fresh lemon juice

♦**INGREDIENT NOTE**
Fresh-squeezed lemon juice has a more lemony punch than reconstituted lemon juice.

PECAN CRISPS

Serve these delicious cookies with coffee-flavored frozen yogurt.

2 tablespoons butter

¼ cup chopped pecans

½ cup sugar

2 large egg whites

⅓ cup all-purpose white flour, sifted

2 teaspoons pure vanilla extract

1. Preheat oven to 300°F. Lightly oil 2 baking sheets or coat them with nonstick cooking spray.

2. In a small saucepan, melt butter over medium heat. Add pecans and stir until the butter is lightly browned and the pecans are toasted, about 1 minute. Transfer to a medium bowl. Whisk in sugar. Add egg whites, flour and vanilla; whisk just until smooth.

3. Drop the batter by rounded teaspoonfuls, 2 inches apart, onto the prepared baking sheets. With the back of a spoon or a small metal spatula, smooth the batter into thin circles 3 inches in diameter. Bake, one sheet at a time, for 10 to 12 minutes, or until golden. Immediately loosen the cookies with a metal spatula.

4. While still hot, remove the cookies from the baking sheet one by one and drape each over a rolling pin. If the cookies become too firm to shape, return them to the oven for about 30 seconds, or until they become pliable. Once the cookies have set, carefully transfer them to a wire rack to finish cooling. (*Store the cookies in an airtight container for up to 3 days. If they lose their crispness, place them in a 350°F oven for about 1 minute, then reshape.*)

Makes about 2 dozen cookies.

40 calories per cookie: 1 gram protein, 2 grams fat (1 gram saturated fat), 6 grams carbohydrate; 15 mg sodium; 3 mg cholesterol.

OATMEAL LACE COOKIES

Thin and elegant, this is a cookie for company.

1. Preheat oven to 400°F. Lightly oil 3 baking sheets or coat them with nonstick cooking spray. Dust them with flour, tapping off the excess.

2. In a bowl, stir together oats, corn syrup and oil. In a small saucepan, melt butter over low heat. Cook, swirling the pan, until the butter turns a nutty brown, about 1 minute. Stir the butter into the oat mixture and set aside.

3. In a mixing bowl, beat egg and sugar with an electric mixer on medium speed until thick and pale, about 5 minutes. Beat in vanilla. In a small bowl, stir together flour, baking powder and salt; fold into the egg mixture. Gently stir in the reserved oat mixture.

4. Drop the batter by teaspoonfuls, about 2 inches apart, onto the prepared baking sheets. Bake, one sheet at a time, for about 5 minutes, or until the cookies are golden and lacy. Let the cookies cool on the baking sheet for about 30 seconds, then carefully transfer them to a flat surface (not a rack) to cool.

5. Place the cookies on a sheet of parchment or wax paper. Pour melted chocolate into a small plastic bag and snip a tiny hole in one corner. Squeeze thin lines of chocolate over the cookies. Let the cookies stand until the chocolate has set, about 1 hour. (*Store in an airtight container with wax paper between the layers for up to 3 days.*)

Makes about 2½ dozen cookies.

50 calories per cookie: 1 gram protein, 2 grams fat (1 gram saturated fat), 7 grams carbohydrate; 41 mg sodium; 9 mg cholesterol.

1	cup rolled oats
⅓	cup light corn syrup
1	tablespoon canola oil
2	tablespoons butter
1	large egg
⅓	cup sugar
1½	teaspoons pure vanilla extract
2	tablespoons all-purpose white flour
1	teaspoon baking powder
¼	teaspoon salt
1	ounce bittersweet (*not unsweetened*) *or* semisweet chocolate, melted

PEANUT BUTTER COOKIES

A healthier version of an old favorite, with much less saturated fat than the original.

2 cups packed light brown sugar

½ cup peanut butter

¼ cup canola oil

2 large eggs

2 teaspoons pure vanilla extract

2 cups all-purpose white flour

⅔ cup whole-wheat flour

1 teaspoon baking powder

1 teaspoon baking soda

½ teaspoon salt

⅓ cup chopped peanuts

1. Preheat oven to 350°F. Lightly oil 3 baking sheets or coat them with nonstick cooking spray.

2. In a mixing bowl, combine brown sugar, peanut butter, oil, eggs and vanilla; add 5 teaspoons water and beat with an electric mixer until smooth. In a small bowl, stir together white and whole-wheat flours, baking powder, baking soda and salt. Stir the dry ingredients into the brown-sugar mixture just until combined.

3. Roll the dough between your palms into 1-inch balls. Place 2 inches apart on the prepared baking sheets. Flatten the cookies with a fork, dipping it into flour if it begins to stick to the dough. Sprinkle with peanuts, pressing them lightly into the dough with your fingers.

4. Bake the cookies, one sheet at a time, for 8 to 10 minutes, or until golden. Transfer to a wire rack to cool. (*Store in an airtight container for up to 3 days.*)

Makes about 4 dozen cookies.

95 calories per cookie: 2 grams protein, 3 grams fat (0 grams saturated fat), 15 grams carbohydrate; 65 mg sodium; 9 mg cholesterol.

◆**SMART SHOPPER**
Choose natural peanut butter because it has no hydrogenated fats.

CHOCOLATE-CHOCOLATE CHIP COOKIES

Soft and chewy, with a deep chocolate flavor.

1. Preheat oven to 350°F. Line 2 or 3 baking sheets with parchment paper. (You may coat the sheets with nonstick cooking spray instead, but the cookies will spread more and have thin and crispy edges.)

2. In a small bowl, stir together flour, cocoa, baking soda and salt; set aside. In a small cup, dissolve coffee powder in vanilla and set aside.

3. Melt butter in a small saucepan over low heat. Cook, swirling the pan, until the butter turns a nutty brown, about 1 minute. Pour into a mixing bowl. Add cream cheese, brown sugar and white sugar. Beat with an electric mixer on low speed until smooth. Add egg and egg white and beat until well incorporated. Add the reserved dry ingredients and dissolved coffee and stir until just combined (the batter will be runny).

4. Drop the batter by slightly rounded tablespoonfuls, 2 inches apart, onto the prepared baking sheets. Sprinkle each cookie with 6 or 7 of the chocolate chips. Bake, one sheet at a time, for 10 to 12 minutes, or until the cookies are puffed and feel "set" when lightly pressed. Slide the parchment paper, with the cookies still attached, onto the counter to cool completely. Gently peel off the paper. (*Store in an airtight container for up to 3 days.*)

Makes about 2½ dozen cookies.

55 calories per cookie: 1 gram protein, 2 grams fat (1 gram saturated fat), 10 grams carbohydrate; 73 mg sodium; 10 mg cholesterol.

¾ cup all-purpose white flour

¼ cup unsweetened cocoa powder, preferably Dutch-process

½ teaspoon baking soda

½ teaspoon salt

1 tablespoon instant coffee powder

2 teaspoons pure vanilla extract

2 tablespoons butter

2 ounces reduced-fat cream cheese (¼ cup)

½ cup packed light brown sugar

⅓ cup white sugar

1 large egg

1 large egg white

½ cup semisweet chocolate chips

MEXICAN MERINGUE COOKIES

These light delights were inspired by Mexican grating chocolate, which is flavored with cinnamon.

½ cup slivered almonds

1 cup sugar

5 tablespoons Dutch-process cocoa powder

3 tablespoons cornstarch

1½ teaspoons ground cinnamon

4 large egg whites

¼ teaspoon cream of tartar

1 teaspoon pure vanilla extract

¼ teaspoon pure almond extract

1½ ounces semisweet *or* bittersweet (*not* unsweetened) chocolate

1. Preheat oven to 350°F. Spread almonds in a pie pan and bake for 5 to 10 minutes, or until lightly toasted. Set aside to cool. Reduce the oven temperature to 200°. Line 2 large baking sheets with parchment paper; set aside.

2. In a food processor, pulse the toasted almonds with ⅓ cup of the sugar until finely chopped. Add cocoa, cornstarch and cinnamon and pulse just until mixed. In a large mixing bowl, beat egg whites with an electric mixer on low speed just until frothy. Add cream of tartar, increase the mixer speed to medium and beat until soft peaks form. Gradually add the remaining ⅔ cup sugar, 2 tablespoons at a time, beating until the whites form firm but still moist peaks. Add vanilla and almond extracts and beat just until blended. In 2 additions, gently fold the cocoa mixture into the beaten whites just until blended. (A few streaks of white may remain.)

3. Drop heaping teaspoonfuls of the batter, 1 inch apart, onto the prepared baking sheets, or pipe the batter through a pastry bag fitted with a ½-inch plain tip. Bake, using both oven racks, for 1½ hours, alternating the positions of the pans halfway through the baking time. Turn off the oven and let the meringues cool in the oven for 1 hour, then peel them off the parchment paper.

4. Melt chocolate in a small bowl set over a pan of almost simmering water or in the microwave. Use a small pastry brush to apply a thin coating of chocolate to the flat side of the meringues. Let the meringues stand, chocolate-side up, until the chocolate has set. (*Store the cookies in an airtight container for up to 5 days.*)

Makes about 4 dozen cookies.

30 calories per cookie: 1 gram protein, 1 gram fat (0 grams saturated fat), 5 grams carbohydrate; 5 mg sodium; 0 mg cholesterol.

Mexican Meringue Cookies

PUMPKIN COOKIES

Moist and cakelike, these gently spiced cookies go well with a glass of milk.

1⅓ cups all-purpose white flour

1 teaspoon baking powder

½ teaspoon baking soda

½ teaspoon salt

1 teaspoon ground cinnamon

½ teaspoon ground ginger

¼ teaspoon ground allspice

¼ teaspoon freshly grated nutmeg

¾ cup canned plain pumpkin puree

¾ cup packed light brown sugar

2 large eggs

¼ cup canola oil

¼ cup dark molasses

1 cup raisins

1. Preheat oven to 350°F. Lightly oil 3 baking sheets or coat them with nonstick cooking spray.

2. In a mixing bowl, whisk together flour, baking powder, baking soda, salt, cinnamon, ginger, allspice and nutmeg. In another bowl, whisk together pumpkin, brown sugar, eggs, oil and molasses until well combined. Stir the wet ingredients and raisins into the dry ingredients until no traces of dry ingredients remain.

3. Drop the batter by level tablespoonfuls onto the prepared baking sheets, spacing the cookies 1½ inches apart. Bake for 10 to 12 minutes, switching the pans midway, or until firm to the touch and lightly golden on top. Transfer the cookies to a wire rack and let cool. (*Store the cookies in an airtight container, with wax paper between the layers, for up to 2 days.*)

Makes about 3 dozen cookies.

70 calories per cookie: 1 gram protein, 2 grams fat (0 grams saturated fat), 13 grams carbohydrate; 56 mg sodium; 12 mg cholesterol.

LUNCHBOX BARS & SQUARES

Bars belong to the no-fuss branch of the baker's repertoire. They can be mixed easily and baked all at once in a single pan. They're sturdy, too, making them ideal for packing into bag lunches or picnic baskets. Mixed with whole grains or studded with dried fruit, these low-fat bars nourish the hungriest student or day hiker, and because they are so low in saturated fat, it's okay to have two.

If you are planning a weekend of outdoor activities, bake a couple of batches on Thursday or Friday night—bars and squares keep well for up to three days in a tightly closed container at room temperature.

RASPBERRIES & CREAM SQUARES

A shortbread base is topped with raspberries swirled with a lemony yogurt "cream."

CRUST

1	cup all-purpose white flour
¼	teaspoon baking powder
¼	teaspoon baking soda
¼	teaspoon salt
½	cup sugar
1	tablespoon butter, softened
1	tablespoon canola oil
1	large egg white
1	teaspoon pure vanilla extract

RASPBERRY LAYER

¼	cup sugar
2	tablespoons cornstarch
12	ounces frozen unsweetened raspberries (3 cups)

"CREAM" LAYER

⅔	cup nonfat sweetened condensed milk
½	cup nonfat plain yogurt
1	large egg
2	tablespoons cornstarch
2	tablespoons fresh lemon juice
1	teaspoon grated lemon zest
1	teaspoon pure vanilla extract

TO MAKE CRUST:

1. Preheat oven to 350°F. Lightly oil an 8-by-12-inch or 7-by-11-inch baking pan or coat it with nonstick cooking spray.

2. In a small bowl, stir together flour, baking powder, baking soda and salt. In a mixing bowl, beat together sugar, butter, oil, egg white and vanilla with an electric mixer until smooth. Stir in the dry ingredients until blended and crumbly.

3. Press the dough into the prepared baking pan in an even layer. Bake the crust for 15 to 20 minutes, or until it is puffed all over and browned around the edges.

TO MAKE RASPBERRY AND CREAM LAYERS:

1. While the bars are baking, stir together sugar and cornstarch in a saucepan. Add raspberries and toss. Stir over medium heat until the mixture is simmering and thickened. When the crust is baked, spread the warm raspberry mixture in an even layer over the crust.

2. In a bowl, whisk together sweetened condensed milk, yogurt, egg, cornstarch, lemon juice, lemon zest and vanilla until smooth; pour over the raspberry layer, tilting the pan to spread it evenly. Drag a fork through the cream layer down into the raspberry layer below to create a marbled effect. Bake for 25 to 30 minutes, or until the filling is puffed and set.

3. Let cool completely in the pan on a wire rack. Cut into squares. (*Store, covered, in the refrigerator for up to 2 days.*)

Makes 20 squares.

115 calories per square: 2 grams protein, 2 grams fat (1 gram saturated fat), 23 grams carbohydrate; 68 mg sodium; 14 mg cholesterol.

TROPICAL FRUIT BARS

Chewy pineapple and papaya, tart lime and sweet coconut combine in an exotic bar.

1. Preheat oven to 350°F. Lightly oil an 8-by-12-inch or 7-by-11-inch baking pan or coat it with nonstick cooking spray

2. In a mixing bowl, whisk together flour, ginger, baking powder, baking soda and salt; set aside. In another bowl, whisk together brown sugar, oil, egg, vanilla and lime zest until no lumps of brown sugar remain. Whisk in lime juice and milk. Add the dry ingredients, pineapple and papaya and stir just until combined.

3. Spread the batter evenly in the prepared pan. Sprinkle coconut over the top. Bake for 20 to 25 minutes, or until golden on top. Let cool completely in the pan on a wire rack. Cut into bars. (*Store at room temperature in an airtight container for up to 3 days.*)

Makes 15 bars.

140 calories per bar: 2 grams protein, 5 grams fat (0 grams saturated fat), 24 grams carbohydrate; 88 mg sodium; 14 mg cholesterol.

1¼	cups sifted cake flour
2	teaspoons ground ginger
½	teaspoon baking powder
½	teaspoon baking soda
¼	teaspoon salt
½	cup packed light brown sugar
¼	cup canola oil
1	large egg
2	teaspoons pure vanilla extract
1	teaspoon grated lime zest
3	tablespoons fresh lime juice
2	tablespoons low-fat milk
¾	cup chopped dried pineapple
¾	cup chopped dried papaya
½	cup flaked sweetened coconut

◆**SMART SHOPPER**
Health-food stores carry many kinds of dried fruits and the price is usually better than at the supermarket.

LEMON SQUARES

While the world clearly doesn't need another recipe for classic lemon squares,
it does need this reduced-fat update; these have a pleasantly tart filling to balance the sweet crust.

CRUST

1	cup all-purpose white flour
¼	teaspoon baking powder
¼	teaspoon baking soda
¼	teaspoon salt
½	cup sugar
1	tablespoon butter, softened
1	tablespoon canola oil
1	large egg white
1	teaspoon grated lemon zest

FILLING

¾	cup sugar
2	teaspoons grated lemon zest
¼	cup fresh lemon juice
1	large egg
1	large egg white
2	tablespoons all-purpose white flour
¼	teaspoon baking powder
	Confectioners' sugar for dusting

TO MAKE CRUST:

1. Preheat oven to 350°F. Lightly oil an 8-by-12-inch or 7-by-11-inch baking pan or coat it with nonstick cooking spray.

2. In a small bowl, stir together flour, baking powder, baking soda and salt. In a mixing bowl, beat together sugar, butter, oil, egg white and lemon zest with an electric mixer until smooth. Stir in the dry ingredients until blended and crumbly.

3. Press the dough in an even layer in the prepared baking pan. Bake the crust for 15 to 20 minutes, or until it is puffed all over and browned around the edges.

TO MAKE FILLING:

Meanwhile, in a bowl, combine sugar, lemon zest and juice, egg, egg white, flour and baking powder; whisk until smooth. Pour evenly over the hot crust and bake for 15 to 20 minutes longer, or until set. Let cool completely in the pan on a wire rack. Cut into squares and dust with confectioners' sugar. (*Store, covered, in the refrigerator for up to 3 days.*)

Makes 18 squares.

100 calories per square: 2 grams protein, 2 grams fat (0.5 grams saturated fat), 20 grams carbohydrate; 67 mg sodium; 14 mg cholesterol.

Lemon Squares

WHOLE-WHEAT BLUEBERRY BARS

A moist fruit filling with a crunchy topping, which is made with the same dough as the crust.

CRUST

1⅓	cups plus about 3 tablespoons whole-wheat pastry flour
½	teaspoon baking powder
½	teaspoon baking soda
½	teaspoon salt
1	cup packed light brown sugar
2	tablespoons butter, softened
2	tablespoons canola oil
1	large egg
1	teaspoon pure vanilla extract

BLUEBERRY FILLING

½	cup white sugar
2	tablespoons all-purpose white flour
1	teaspoon grated lemon zest
2	cups fresh *or* frozen unsweetened blueberries
1	tablespoon fresh lemon juice
	Confectioners' sugar for dusting (optional)

◆**SMART SHOPPER**

Whole-wheat pastry flour is available at health-food stores and large supermarkets; the bars can also be made with all-purpose white flour.

TO MAKE CRUST:

1. Preheat oven to 350°F. Lightly oil an 8-by-12-inch or 7-by-11-inch baking pan or coat it with nonstick cooking spray; set aside.

2. In a large bowl, whisk together 1⅓ cups of the flour, baking powder, baking soda and salt. In another bowl, beat together brown sugar, butter, oil, egg and vanilla with an electric mixer on high speed until smooth, making sure no lumps of brown sugar remain, about 1 minute. Add the dry ingredients and stir with a wooden spoon until well blended. The dough will be quite firm.

3. Transfer two-thirds of the dough to the prepared baking pan; cover the dough with a piece of plastic wrap and use it to press the dough into the bottom of the pan in an even layer. Remove the plastic wrap. Bake for 15 minutes, or until puffed and golden.

4. Using your fingertips, gradually work enough of the remaining 3 tablespoons flour into the remaining dough until it resembles coarse crumbs; set aside to use as the topping.

TO MAKE FILLING:

1. In a small bowl, stir together the sugar, flour and lemon zest. In a saucepan, combine blueberries and lemon juice; cook, stirring, over medium heat until the berries begin to exude juice. Add the sugar mixture and stir until the filling reaches a simmer and thickens.

2. With a wooden spoon, push down the higher outside edges of the baked crust; pour the hot filling over it and spread all the way to the sides of the pan. Sprinkle the crumb topping over the top. Bake for 15 to 20 minutes longer, or until the topping is golden.

3. Transfer the baking pan to a wire rack and let cool, covered with a kitchen towel to soften the crumbs slightly. Cut into bars. If desired, dust lightly with confectioners' sugar. (*Store, covered, in the refrigerator for up to 3 days.*)

Makes 15 bars.

170 calories per bar: 2 grams protein, 4 grams fat (1 gram saturated fat), 33 grams carbohydrate; 135 mg sodium; 18 mg cholesterol.

CRANBERRY-GRANOLA BLONDIES

Packed with dried fruit and cereal, these firm bars are excellent travelers.

1. Preheat oven to 350°F. Lightly oil a 9-by-13-inch baking pan or coat it with nonstick cooking spray; set aside.

2. In a small bowl, whisk together flour, baking powder and salt. In a large bowl, beat together brown sugar, oil and egg whites with an electric mixer on high speed until smooth, making sure no lumps of brown sugar remain. Add the dry ingredients and beat on low speed just until blended. Stir in granola and dried fruit. (The batter will be quite thick.)

3. Transfer the batter to the prepared baking pan; smooth the top. Bake for 20 to 25 minutes, or until the blondies are golden brown on top and feel "set" when lightly pressed in the center.

4. Let cool in the baking pan on a wire rack. Cut into bars. (*Store at room temperature in an airtight container for up to 3 days.*)

Makes 20 bars.

150 calories per bar: 2 grams protein, 3 grams fat (0 grams saturated fat), 29 grams carbohydrate; 103 mg sodium; 0 mg cholesterol.

1   cup all-purpose white flour

1   teaspoon baking powder

½   teaspoon salt

1¼   cups packed light brown sugar

¼   cup canola oil

3   large egg whites

2   cups low-fat granola cereal with raisins

1   cup dried cranberries *or* chopped dried tart cherries

◆ **GETTING AHEAD**

Bake bars in an aluminum-foil pan; cool, then freeze the whole thing. Alternatively, line a glass or metal baking dish with enough foil to come well up over the edges; once the bars have cooled, lift out the entire uncut layer, wrap and freeze for up to 2 months.

CHOCOLATE CHIP BARS

A bar version of the classic cookie, these slightly chewy confections are a delight.

⅔ cup all-purpose white flour

½ teaspoon baking soda

½ teaspoon salt

2 tablespoons butter

2 ounces reduced-fat cream cheese (¼ cup)

½ cup packed light brown sugar

½ cup white sugar

1 large egg

1½ teaspoons pure vanilla extract

½ cup semisweet chocolate chips, coarsely chopped, *or* mini chocolate chips

1. Preheat oven to 375°F. Lightly oil an 8-by-12-inch or 7-by-11-inch baking pan or coat it with nonstick cooking spray. Set aside.

2. In a mixing bowl, stir together flour, baking soda and salt; set aside. Melt butter in a small saucepan over low heat. Cook, swirling the pan, until the butter turns a nutty brown, 30 to 60 seconds. Pour into a large mixing bowl. Add cream cheese, brown sugar and white sugar. Beat with an electric mixer on low speed until smooth. Add egg and vanilla; beat until well incorporated. Add the reserved dry ingredients and chocolate chips and stir just until combined.

3. Pour the batter into the prepared baking pan and bake for 20 to 25 minutes, or until a skewer inserted in the center comes out clean. Let cool completely in the pan on a wire rack. Cut into bars. (*Store at room temperature in an airtight container for up to 3 days.*)

Makes 15 bars.

115 calories per bar: 2 grams protein, 4 grams fat (1.5 grams saturated fat), 21 grams carbohydrate; 142 mg sodium; 20 mg cholesterol.

HERMITS

These moist, spicy favorites keep well (if they get the chance).

1. Preheat oven to 350°F. Lightly oil a 9-by-13-inch baking pan or coat it with nonstick cooking spray; set aside.

2. In a small bowl, whisk together flour, baking powder, baking soda, salt, cinnamon, allspice, nutmeg and cloves. In a large bowl, beat together molasses, brown sugar, oil, apple butter and eggs with an electric mixer until smooth. Add the dry ingredients and beat on low speed just until combined. Stir in raisins. Transfer the batter to the prepared baking pan; smooth the top. Bake for 20 to 25 minutes, or until the batter feels "set" when lightly pressed in the center.

3. Let cool in the baking pan on a rack. Cut into bars. (*Store at room temperature in an airtight container for up to 3 days.*)

Makes 20 bars.

155 calories per bar: 2 grams protein, 3 grams fat (1 gram saturated fat), 30 grams carbohydrate; 102 mg sodium; 21 mg cholesterol.

1⅓ cups all-purpose white flour

1 teaspoon baking powder

½ teaspoon baking soda

½ teaspoon salt

2 teaspoons ground cinnamon

1 teaspoon ground allspice

½ teaspoon freshly grated nutmeg

¼ teaspoon ground cloves

½ cup dark molasses

¾ cup packed light brown sugar

¼ cup canola oil

¼ cup apple butter

2 large eggs

1½ cups raisins

♦INGREDIENT NOTE
Spices lose their punch over time. Start with fresh ones each year.

FIG BARS

Better than their store-bought cousins, these bars have a richly flavored filling, with a little bit of crispness to the crust.

FILLING

1	cup packed chopped dried figs, stems removed
1	tablespoon fresh lemon juice
1	teaspoon grated lemon zest
⅛	teaspoon salt

DOUGH

1⅓	cups all-purpose white flour
½	teaspoon baking powder
½	teaspoon baking soda
½	teaspoon salt
1	cup packed light brown sugar
2	tablespoons butter, softened
2	tablespoons canola oil
1	large egg
1	teaspoon pure vanilla extract
	Confectioners' sugar for dusting (optional)

◆**LOW-FAT BAKING TIP**

Doughs for reduced-fat pastries can tend to be sticky, but pressing them out under a piece of plastic wrap or wax paper easily solves the problem.

TO MAKE FILLING:

In a saucepan, stir together figs, ½ cup water, lemon juice, lemon zest and salt. Bring to a simmer and stir over low heat until thickened, about 3 minutes. Transfer to a food processor and puree until smooth; set aside to cool to lukewarm.

TO MAKE DOUGH AND ASSEMBLE BARS:

1. Preheat oven to 350°F. In a small bowl, stir together flour, baking powder, baking soda and salt. In a large bowl, beat together brown sugar, butter, oil, egg and vanilla with an electric mixer on high speed until smooth, making sure no lumps of brown sugar remain, about 1 minute. Add the dry ingredients and stir with a wooden spoon until completely blended. (The dough will be stiff.)

2. To shape the dough, line the bottom of an 8-by-12-inch or 7-by-11-inch baking pan with a piece of plastic wrap; smooth out any wrinkles. Evenly press one-half of the dough into the bottom of the lined pan. If the dough is sticky, smooth it out under another piece of plastic wrap. Pick up the ends of the plastic wrap and lift out the piece of dough.

3. Lightly oil the bottom of the same baking pan or coat it with non-stick cooking spray. Press the remaining half of the dough into the pan. Spread the fig filling on top. Invert the first half of the dough onto the filling and peel away the plastic wrap. Bake for 25 to 30 minutes, or until the upper crust appears completely baked when pierced in the center with a skewer.

4. Transfer the baking pan to a wire rack and let cool, covered with a kitchen towel to help soften the top crust. Cut into bars. If desired, dust lightly with confectioners' sugar. (*Store at room temperature in an airtight container for up to 3 days.*)

Makes 15 bars.

170 calories per bar: 2 grams protein, 4 grams fat (1 gram saturated fat), 33 grams carbohydrate; 153 mg sodium; 18 mg cholesterol.

Apricot-Oatmeal Bars

APRICOT-OATMEAL BARS

These pretty streusel-topped bars are quick to make and easy to transport.
Made with unsweetened apricot preserves, they are a good source of potassium and beta carotene.

1. Preheat oven to 325°F. Lightly oil an 8-by-12-inch or 7-by-11-inch baking pan or coat it with nonstick cooking spray; set aside.

2. In a large bowl, work together oats, flour, brown sugar, salt and baking soda with your fingertips until no lumps of brown sugar remain. Drizzle oil and fruit juice over the oats and mix in until evenly moistened and crumbly. Set aside ½ cup for the topping; press the remainder evenly into the prepared baking pan. Spread apricot preserves over the top. Sprinkle with the reserved oat topping.

3. Bake for 30 to 40 minutes, or until golden. Let cool in the baking pan on a wire rack. Cut into bars. (*Store at room temperature in an airtight container for up to 3 days.*)

Makes 15 bars.

195 calories per bar: 3 grams protein, 4 grams fat (1 gram saturated fat), 36 grams carbohydrate; 55 mg sodium; 0 mg cholesterol.

1 cup "quick" rolled oats

1 cup all-purpose white flour

⅔ cup packed light brown sugar

¼ teaspoon salt

¼ teaspoon baking soda

¼ cup canola oil

3 tablespoons apple *or* cranberry juice

1 10-ounce jar apricot preserves, preferably "all-fruit" (1 scant cup)

DATE-PECAN BARS

Here, graham cracker crumbs and dates are folded into beaten eggs and sugar to make
a wonderfully chewy date bar, with a fraction of the fat of traditional recipes.

2	teaspoons instant espresso *or* coffee powder
2	teaspoons pure vanilla extract
¾	cup sugar
2	large eggs
1	large egg white
¼	teaspoon salt
2	cups fine graham cracker crumbs (18 whole crackers)
⅔	cup chopped dates
½	cup chopped pecans
	Confectioners' sugar for dusting (optional)

1. Preheat oven to 300°F. Lightly oil an 8-by-12-inch or 7-by-11-inch baking pan or coat it with nonstick cooking spray; set aside.

2. In a large mixing bowl, stir together coffee powder and vanilla until the powder dissolves; add sugar, eggs, egg white and salt and beat with an electric mixer on high speed until thick and pale, about 2 minutes. With a rubber spatula, fold in graham cracker crumbs, dates and pecans just until combined.

3. Transfer the batter to the prepared baking pan; smooth the top. Bake for 30 to 35 minutes, or until the top feels dry and a skewer inserted in the center comes out clean.

4. Let cool in the baking pan on a wire rack. Cut into bars. If desired, dust lightly with confectioners' sugar. (*Store at room temperature in an airtight container for up to 3 days.*)

Makes 15 bars.

130 calories per bar: 2 grams protein, 4 grams fat (1 gram saturated fat), 23 grams carbohydrate; 88 mg sodium; 28 mg cholesterol.

◆**BAKING TIP**
Turn graham crackers into crumbs in the food processor.
Or place the crackers between two sheets of wax paper and roll them with a rolling pin.

PROPER SCONES & TEA CAKES

There's a point in the day when you need something sweet, but not too sweet, to go with a cup of tea or coffee. This collection of scones, muffins and coffee and tea cakes satisfies just that need. There is even a doughnut recipe. Actually, the doughnuts are little cakes baked in mini-Bundt pans, but they look and taste like real cake doughnuts: instead of a dozen or more grams of fat in each one, they contain just four. Any of these scrumptious and easy baked goods will make for a healthful break during a hectic day.

Cranberry-Walnut Scones

CRANBERRY-WALNUT SCONES

In the unlikely event you have any scones left over, toast them to recrisp the outer crust before serving.

1. Preheat oven to 425°F. Lightly oil a baking sheet or coat it with nonstick cooking spray.

2. In a large bowl, stir together flour, ¼ cup brown sugar, baking powder and salt. With a pastry blender or your fingertips, cut in butter until the mixture resembles coarse crumbs. Stir in cranberries and walnuts. Make a well in the center and gradually stir in buttermilk to form a ball. Knead lightly. Do not overwork; the dough will be sticky.

3. Divide the dough in half. On a lightly floured surface, pat or roll each portion into an 8-inch round, about ½ inch thick. Cut each round into 8 triangles. Place the scones on the prepared baking sheet. Brush the tops with buttermilk and sprinkle with the remaining 1 tablespoon brown sugar. Bake for 14 to 18 minutes, or until golden brown. Serve warm.

Makes 16 scones.

115 calories per serving: 3 grams protein, 3 grams fat (1 gram saturated fat), 21 grams carbohydrate; 140 mg sodium; 4 mg cholesterol.

- 2 cups all-purpose white flour
- ¼ cup light brown sugar, plus 1 tablespoon for sprinkling scone tops
- 2 teaspoons baking powder
- ½ teaspoon salt
- 2 tablespoons unsalted butter
- ½ cup fresh *or* dried cranberries
- ¼ cup chopped walnuts
- 1 cup buttermilk, plus extra for brushing scone tops

ORANGE-RAISIN SCONES

Golden, moist and tender with a cakelike texture, these are the perfect excuse for a coffee or tea break.

- 2 cups all-purpose white flour
- ¼ cup sugar
- 1 teaspoon baking powder
- 1 teaspoon baking soda
- ½ teaspoon salt
- ¾ cup coarsely chopped raisins *or* whole currants
- 1 tablespoon butter
- 2 tablespoons canola oil
- 1 cup nonfat plain yogurt, plus extra for brushing scone tops
- 1 large egg
- 1 tablespoon grated orange zest

1. Preheat oven to 375°F. Lightly oil a baking sheet or coat it with nonstick cooking spray; set aside.

2. In a mixing bowl, stir together flour, sugar, baking powder, baking soda and salt. Add raisins or currants, tossing to coat. In a small saucepan, melt butter over low heat. Cook, swirling the pan, until it turns a nutty brown, about 1 minute. Transfer the butter to a bowl. Add oil, 1 cup yogurt, egg and orange zest and whisk until blended. Add the yogurt mixture to the dry ingredients, stirring just until combined (the dough will be sticky).

3. Transfer the dough to the prepared baking sheet; with floured hands, pat it out into a ½-inch-thick circle. Cut the circle into 12 wedges, leaving them in place. Brush the top with yogurt.

4. Bake for 15 to 20 minutes, or until the top is golden and firm to the touch. Serve warm.

Makes 1 dozen scones.

165 calories per scone: 4 grams protein, 4 grams fat (1 gram saturated fat), 29 grams carbohydrate; 216 mg sodium; 21 mg cholesterol.

SPICED COFFEE CAKE WITH PEARS

Fragrant pears bake under a gingerbread batter, making for a lovely presentation with a minimum of effort.

1. Position rack in the lower third of the oven; preheat to 375°F. Lightly oil an 8-inch square baking dish or coat it with nonstick cooking spray.

2. Pour butter into the prepared baking dish and tilt to coat the bottom evenly. Sprinkle brown sugar over the butter. Peel, halve and core pears. Brush with lemon juice. Cut a pear half crosswise into ⅛-inch-thick slices. Holding the slices together, slide a metal spatula underneath and invert the sliced pear half onto your hand, pressing to fan slightly. Place it, rounded-side down, on the brown sugar in the baking dish. Repeat with the remaining pear halves. Bake, uncovered, for 15 minutes.

3. Meanwhile, whisk flour, baking powder, baking soda, salt, cinnamon, ginger, allspice and nutmeg in a bowl; stir in white sugar. In a large bowl, whisk together egg whites, buttermilk, molasses and oil. Add the dry ingredients to the wet ingredients and stir just until blended.

4. When the pears have baked for 15 minutes, pour the batter evenly over the top. Bake for 30 to 35 minutes longer, or until a skewer inserted in the center comes out clean. Loosen the edges. Invert a serving plate on top of the baking pan and, grasping firmly with hands protected with oven mitts, quickly turn the cake and plate over. Remove the baking dish. Remove any pear slices that adhere to the dish and replace them on top of the cake. Let cool for at least 10 minutes, cut into squares and serve warm.

Serves 9.

215 calories per serving: 3 grams protein, 5 grams fat (1 gram saturated fat), 42 grams carbohydrate; 225 mg sodium; 4 mg cholesterol.

1	tablespoon butter, melted
3	tablespoons light brown sugar
3	ripe but firm pears, such as Bartlett *or* Bosc
1	tablespoon fresh lemon juice
1¼	cups sifted cake flour
½	teaspoon baking powder
½	teaspoon baking soda
½	teaspoon salt
2	teaspoons ground cinnamon
1	teaspoon ground ginger
½	teaspoon ground allspice
¼	teaspoon freshly grated nutmeg
½	cup white sugar
2	large egg whites
½	cup buttermilk
¼	cup dark molasses
2	tablespoons canola oil

◆**BAKING TIP**

Where things are baked in the oven will have a dramatic effect on the final outcome. If you're after a well-browned bottom, set the shelf in the lower third of the oven. For a golden top, use the upper position instead.

BLUEBERRY COFFEE CAKE

For the best texture, do not overmix the batter or the cake will be tough.

CAKE

1	large egg
½	cup skim milk
½	cup nonfat plain yogurt
3	tablespoons canola oil
2	cups all-purpose white flour
½	cup sugar
4	teaspoons baking powder
½	teaspoon salt
1½	cups fresh *or* frozen unsweetened blueberries

TOPPING

3	tablespoons sugar
2	tablespoons finely chopped walnuts
¼	teaspoon ground cinnamon

TO MAKE CAKE:

1. Preheat oven to 400°F. Lightly oil an 8-inch square baking dish or coat it with nonstick cooking spray.

2. In a large mixing bowl, whisk together egg, milk, yogurt and oil. Set a sieve on top of the bowl and measure flour, sugar, baking powder and salt into it. Stir the dry ingredients together while sifting them into the liquid mixture. Stir the batter just to blend. Do not overmix. Fold in blueberries. Transfer the batter to the prepared pan.

TO PREPARE TOPPING & BAKE CAKE:

1. In a small bowl, stir together sugar, walnuts and cinnamon; sprinkle over the batter.

2. Bake for 20 to 25 minutes, or until the top is golden brown and a skewer inserted in the center comes out clean. (Add about 20 minutes to the baking time if using frozen berries.) Let cool in the pan on a wire rack for 10 minutes. Cut into squares and serve warm.

Serves 9.

240 calories per serving: 5 grams protein, 6 grams fat (1 gram saturated fat), 42 grams carbohydrate; 290 mg sodium; 24 mg cholesterol.

◆**GETTING AHEAD**

To save time in the morning, measure out and mix the dry ingredients the night before. Although they are best when fresh baked, coffee cakes also can be baked ahead and frozen. Defrost and warm in the oven or microwave.

PRUNE COFFEE CAKE

The delicious blending of dark, sweet prunes with a light touch of spices will make a prune lover out of almost anyone.

1. Preheat oven to 350°F. Lightly oil an 8-inch square baking pan or coat it with nonstick cooking spray.

2. In a food processor, combine ⅔ cup of the prunes and ⅓ cup hot water; process until smooth. Coarsely chop the remaining ⅔ cup prunes. Set the prune puree and chopped prunes aside.

3. In a medium bowl, whisk flour, baking powder, baking soda, salt, cinnamon, nutmeg and cloves. In a small bowl, toss 1 tablespoon of the dry ingredients with the chopped prunes. In a mixing bowl, combine the reserved prune puree, 1 cup sugar, egg whites, yogurt, oil and vanilla; beat with an electric mixer on medium speed until blended. In 3 additions, add the dry ingredients to the batter, beating on low speed between additions. Occasionally, stop and scrape down the bowl and beater with a rubber spatula. Stir in the flour-coated chopped prunes.

4. Turn the batter into the prepared pan and sprinkle 1½ tablespoons sugar evenly over the top. Bake for 35 to 40 minutes, or until a skewer inserted in the center comes out clean. Let cool in the pan on a wire rack for at least 10 minutes. Cut into squares and serve warm.

Serves 9.

295 calories per serving: 4 grams protein, 6 grams fat (1 gram saturated fat), 57 grams carbohydrate; 247 mg sodium; 0 mg cholesterol.

1⅓	cups pitted prunes
1¾	cups sifted cake flour
1½	teaspoons baking powder
½	teaspoon baking soda
½	teaspoon salt
1½	teaspoons ground cinnamon
½	teaspoon ground nutmeg
¼	teaspoon ground cloves
1	cup plus 1½ tablespoons sugar
2	large egg whites
¾	cup nonfat plain yogurt
¼	cup canola oil
1	teaspoon pure vanilla extract

ORANGE MARMALADE COFFEE CAKE

Instead of coffee, make some not-too-sweet hot chocolate to serve with the orangy cake.

1 large egg

1 cup low-fat lemon or orange yogurt

3 tablespoons canola oil

3 tablespoons fresh orange juice

1 tablespoon grated orange zest

2 teaspoons pure vanilla extract

2¼ cups sifted cake flour

½ cup sugar

1 tablespoon baking powder

½ teaspoon salt

¼ teaspoon baking soda

¾ cup orange marmalade

1. Preheat oven to 350°F. Lightly oil an 8-inch square baking pan or coat it with nonstick cooking spray.

2. In a large bowl, whisk together egg, yogurt, oil, orange juice, orange zest and vanilla. In another bowl, stir together flour, sugar, baking powder, salt and baking soda. Add the dry ingredients to the egg mixture and stir just until blended.

3. Transfer the batter to the prepared pan and bake for 30 to 35 minutes, or until a skewer inserted in the center comes out clean. Cool in the pan on a wire rack for 10 minutes.

4. In a small saucepan, heat marmalade over medium heat; simmer, stirring constantly, until slightly thickened, about 6 minutes. Spoon over the cake, spreading evenly. Let cool slightly, cut into squares and serve warm.

Serves 9.

295 calories per serving: 4 grams protein, 6 grams fat (1 gram saturated fat), 57 grams carbohydrate; 276 mg sodium; 25 mg cholesterol.

◆**INGREDIENT NOTE**

Choose a good imported marmalade made from Seville oranges.
Their bittersweet quality balances the moist, rich cake.

QUICK CINNAMON ROLLS

The best thing to have on a chilly afternoon.

TO MAKE CINNAMON ROLLS:

1. Preheat oven to 400°F. Lightly oil an 8-inch square baking dish or coat it with nonstick cooking spray.

2. In a small bowl, pour ¼ cup boiling water over raisins; cover and set aside. In another bowl, whisk together flour, baking powder and salt; set aside. In a third bowl, mix together brown sugar and cinnamon and set aside.

3. In a food processor, puree cottage cheese. Add white sugar, milk, oil and vanilla and process until very smooth. Add the flour mixture and pulse 4 or 5 times, just until the dough clumps together. Turn out onto a work surface and knead several times to make a soft dough. Dust the dough and work surface with flour and roll into a rectangle, approximately 15 by 10 inches.

4. Brush the dough with melted butter, leaving a ½-inch border around the perimeter. Sprinkle with the brown-sugar mixture; run the rolling pin over the surface to gently press the sugar into the dough. Drain any liquid from the raisins and sprinkle them over the sugar. Starting at a long edge, roll up, jelly-roll fashion. Pinch the edges of the dough together along the seam. With a sharp knife, trim the ends. Slice the dough into 12 rolls. Set the rolls, cut-side up, in the prepared baking dish. (The rolls will fill the dish as they bake.) Bake for 25 to 30 minutes, or until golden and firm to the touch. Loosen the edges and invert onto a wire rack to cool slightly. Turn the rolls right-side up for glazing.

TO MAKE GLAZE:

In a small bowl, whisk together the confectioners' sugar, vanilla and just enough milk to make a nice consistency for drizzling. Drizzle the glaze over the rolls and serve warm.

Makes 1 dozen rolls.

220 calories per roll: 4 grams protein, 6 grams fat (1 gram saturated fat), 38 grams carbohydrate; 20 mg sodium; 3 mg cholesterol.

CINNAMON ROLLS

- ½ cup raisins
- 2 cups all-purpose white flour
- 1 tablespoon baking powder
- ¼ teaspoon salt
- ⅓ cup packed brown sugar
- 2 teaspoons ground cinnamon
- ¾ cup low-fat cottage cheese
- ⅓ cup white sugar
- ⅓ cup low-fat milk
- ¼ cup canola oil
- 1½ teaspoons pure vanilla extract
- 1 tablespoon butter, melted

GLAZE

- ½ cup confectioners' sugar,
- 1 teaspoon pure vanilla extract
- 2-3 teaspoons low-fat milk

APRICOT & GOLDEN RAISIN TEA LOAF

Full of tart flavor, this quick bread is great for toasting.

¼ cup chopped hazelnuts (filberts)

1¼ cups dried apricots, chopped

2½ cups all-purpose white flour

½ cup sugar

2 teaspoons baking powder

1 teaspoon baking soda

½ teaspoon salt

1 large egg

2 large egg whites

⅔ cup buttermilk

3 tablespoons hazelnut oil *or* canola oil

1 teaspoon pure vanilla extract

¾ cup golden raisins

1. Preheat oven to 350°F. Lightly oil a 9-by-5-inch loaf pan or coat it with nonstick cooking spray; set aside. Spread hazelnuts on a baking sheet and bake for 5 minutes, or until lightly toasted; let cool.

2. In a small saucepan, combine ½ cup of the apricots with ½ cup water. Bring to a simmer, remove from the heat and let stand for 10 minutes. Transfer the apricots and their liquid to a food processor and process until they form a chunky puree; set aside (you should have about ½ cup puree).

3. In a large bowl, stir together flour, sugar, baking powder, baking soda and salt. In another large bowl, whisk together egg, egg whites, buttermilk, oil, vanilla and the reserved apricot puree until smooth. Stir the apricot mixture into the dry ingredients just until combined. Fold in raisins, hazelnuts and the remaining ¾ cup apricots. Turn the batter out into the prepared pan, smoothing the top.

4. Bake for 50 to 60 minutes, or until the top is golden and a skewer inserted in the center of the loaf comes out clean. Let cool in the pan for 10 minutes. Loosen the edges and invert the loaf onto a wire rack to cool. Serve warm or at room temperature.

Makes 1 loaf, 12 slices.

260 calories per slice: 6 grams protein, 7 grams fat (1 gram saturated fat), 45 grams carbohydrate; 245 mg sodium; 18 mg cholesterol.

◆**STORAGE NOTE**

After opening, store hazelnut oil, or any other nut oil, in the refrigerator to keep it from going rancid.

Apricot & Golden Raisin Tea Loaf

ZUCCHINI BREAD

Not too sweet, and very fragrant, this is good bread to bake if you're trying to sell your house.

1	cup rolled oats
½	cup pecan halves
2¼	cups all-purpose white flour
1½	cups whole-wheat pastry flour
1½	tablespoons baking powder
2	teaspoons ground cinnamon
½	teaspoon freshly grated nutmeg
¼	teaspoon ground cloves
1½	teaspoons salt
2	cups packed light brown sugar
2	large eggs
2	large egg whites
¾	cup apple butter
⅓	cup canola oil
3	cups grated zucchini (about 2 small zucchini)

1. Preheat oven to 350°F. Lightly oil two 9-by-5-inch loaf pans or coat them with nonstick cooking spray. Spread oats and pecans on separate parts of a baking sheet and bake for 5 to 10 minutes, or until lightly toasted; let cool. Chop the pecans.

2. In a mixing bowl, stir together all but 2 tablespoons of the toasted oats, the pecans, white and whole-wheat flours, baking powder, cinnamon, nutmeg, cloves and salt. In another bowl, whisk together brown sugar, eggs, egg whites, apple butter and oil; stir in zucchini. Stir this mixture into the dry ingredients just until well combined.

3. Divide the batter between the prepared loaf pans, smoothing the tops. Sprinkle 1 tablespoon of the reserved oats on top of each loaf. Bake for 45 to 55 minutes, or until the tops feel firm when lightly pressed and a skewer inserted in the center comes out clean.

4. Let the loaves rest in the pans for 5 minutes; turn them out onto a wire rack to cool completely.

Makes 2 loaves, 12 slices per loaf.

220 calories per slice: 4 grams protein, 6 grams fat (1 gram saturated fat), 40 grams carbohydrate; 212 mg sodium; 18 mg cholesterol.

PUMPKIN & CRANBERRY BREAD

Cornmeal gives this moist quick bread a subtle crunch.

1. Preheat oven to 350°F. Lightly oil two 9-by-5-inch loaf pans or coat them with nonstick cooking spray; dust with flour and tap out the excess.

2. In a mixing bowl, combine white and whole-wheat flours, cornmeal, brown sugar, baking powder, baking soda, cinnamon, ginger and salt; mix well, breaking up any lumps of brown sugar with your fingertips. In another bowl, whisk together pumpkin, yogurt, oil, eggs and egg whites until well combined. Stir the pumpkin mixture and cranberries or raisins into the dry ingredients until completely blended, but do not overmix.

3. Divide the batter between the loaf pans, smoothing the tops with a spatula. Bake for 55 to 65 minutes, or until a skewer inserted in the center comes out clean.

4. Let the loaves rest in the pans for 5 minutes; turn them out onto a wire rack to cool completely.

Makes 2 loaves, 12 slices per loaf.

200 calories per slice: 3 grams protein, 4 grams fat (1 gram saturated fat), 40 grams carbohydrate; 224 mg sodium; 18 mg cholesterol.

- 1 cup all-purpose white flour
- 1 cup whole-wheat flour
- 1 cup cornmeal, preferably stone-ground
- 2 cups packed brown sugar
- 1 tablespoon baking powder
- 2 teaspoons baking soda
- 2 teaspoons ground cinnamon
- 1 teaspoon ground ginger
- 1 teaspoon salt
- 1 15- or 16-ounce can plain pumpkin puree (1½ cups)
- 1 cup nonfat plain yogurt
- ⅓ cup canola oil
- 2 large eggs
- 2 large egg whites
- 2 cups dried cranberries *or* raisins

♦**INGREDIENT NOTE**
"Stone-ground" cornmeal includes the germ and some of the hull, so it's more nutritious and has a more interesting texture. Store it in the freezer.

APPLE-CIDER "DOUGHNUTS" WITH MAPLE GLAZE

This recipe was inspired by two treats you find while touring Vermont (home of EATING WELL*): cider doughnuts and maple syrup.*

3 tablespoons white sugar (approximately) for preparing pans

2 cups all-purpose white flour

1½ teaspoons baking powder

1½ teaspoons baking soda

½ teaspoon salt

2 teaspoons ground cinnamon

1 large egg, lightly beaten

⅔ cup packed brown sugar

½ cup apple butter

⅓ cup pure maple syrup

⅓ cup apple cider

⅓ cup nonfat plain yogurt

3 tablespoons canola oil

MAPLE GLAZE

1¼ cups confectioners' sugar

1 teaspoon pure vanilla extract

¼-⅓ cup pure maple syrup

1. Preheat oven to 400°F. Coat the molds of a mini-Bundt pan with nonstick cooking spray or oil. Sprinkle with white sugar, shaking out the excess.

2. In a mixing bowl, whisk together flour, baking powder, baking soda, salt and cinnamon; set aside. In another bowl, whisk together egg, brown sugar, apple butter, maple syrup, cider, yogurt and oil. Add the dry ingredients and stir just until moistened. Divide half the batter among the prepared molds, spooning about 2 generous tablespoonfuls of batter into each mold.

3. Bake for 10 to 12 minutes, or until the tops spring back when touched lightly. Loosen the edges and turn the cakes out onto a wire rack to cool. Clean the mini-Bundt pan, then recoat it with cooking spray or oil and sugar. Repeat with the remaining batter.

TO MAKE MAPLE GLAZE:

In a bowl, combine confectioners' sugar and vanilla. Gradually whisk in enough maple syrup to make a coating consistency. Dip the fluted side of the "doughnuts" in the glaze to coat. Then set them glazed-side up on a wire rack over wax paper for a few minutes until the glaze has set.

Makes 1 dozen doughnuts.

285 calories per doughnut: 3 grams protein, 4 grams fat (0 grams saturated fat), 61 grams carbohydrate; 263 mg sodium; 18 mg cholesterol.

◆**EQUIPMENT NOTE**

Coating a mold or cake pan with sugar before adding the batter will give the outside of the cake an appealing crisp glaze. A mini-Bundt pan produces adorable doughnut-shaped cakes, but if you do not have one, you can use a regular Bundt pan and make a coffee cake; bake it in a 375°F oven for 25 to 30 minutes.

Apple-Cider "Doughnuts" with Maple Glaze

RHUBARB MUFFINS

A sweet treat from the Inn at the Round Barn Farm in Waitsfield, Vermont.

¼ cup sugar

½ teaspoon ground cinnamon

3 tablespoons finely chopped pecans

1 cup buttermilk

1 large egg

1 cup packed light brown sugar

¼ cup canola oil

1½ teaspoons pure vanilla extract

1½ cups diced rhubarb

1¾ cups all-purpose white flour

1 teaspoon baking powder

1 teaspoon baking soda

½ teaspoon salt

1. Preheat oven to 400°F. Lightly oil 12 muffin cups or coat with nonstick cooking spray; set aside. In a small bowl, stir together sugar, cinnamon and nuts; set aside.

2. In a mixing bowl, whisk together buttermilk, egg, brown sugar, oil, and vanilla until smooth; stir in rhubarb. In another bowl, whisk together flour, baking powder, baking soda and salt; add to the buttermilk/rhubarb mixture and stir until just combined.

3. Spoon the batter into the prepared muffin cups. Sprinkle the reserved sugar/nut mixture over the tops of the muffins. Bake for 20 to 25 minutes, or until the muffins are golden brown. Let cool briefly on a wire rack before serving.

Makes 1 dozen muffins.

220 calories per muffin: 3 grams protein, 6 grams fat (1 gram saturated fat), 38 grams carbohydrate; 218 mg sodium; 19 mg cholesterol.

◆**VARIATION**

Add 2 tablespoons "quick" rolled oats to the topping for a little crunch.

ICE CREAMS & OTHER FROZEN DELIGHTS

The average American eats more than four gallons of ice cream and frozen yogurt every year. Yet the first spoonful of the frosty stuff always brings a special delight that seems rooted in long-ago childhood summers. These days, it's a joy to make ice cream, ices and sorbets. Homemade ice cream used to require layering coarse salt and cracked ice in an ice cream maker and cranking until you could crank no more. The introduction in the 1980s of compact ice cream makers whose cooling units fit into the freezer changed all that.

VANILLA ICE CREAM

Commercial marshmallow creme is the short-cut secret to this ice cream's velvety texture.
The brand we use is Marshmallow Fluff.

4 cups skim milk

¼ cup corn syrup

3 large egg yolks

¼ cup cornstarch

2½ cups marshmallow creme, such as Fluff

2 tablespoons pure vanilla extract, preferably Madagascar

◆TOP-NOTCH VANILLA

For the fullest vanilla flavor, choose a top-quality extract. Bourbon vanilla beans from Madagascar are among the finest, and extracts labeled Madagascar Bourbon Vanilla are rich and aromatic.

1. In a large heavy saucepan, combine 3¾ cups of the milk and corn syrup. Heat over medium heat, stirring to dissolve the corn syrup, until steaming. Meanwhile, in a mixing bowl, whisk together egg yolks, cornstarch and the remaining ¼ cup cold milk until smooth. Gradually whisk 1 cup hot milk into the egg-yolk mixture; then pour the egg-yolk mixture into the hot milk in the pan. Cook over medium heat, whisking constantly, until the mixture boils and thickens, 3 to 5 minutes. (Because the custard is thickened with cornstarch, it will not curdle when it boils.)

2. Transfer the custard to a large clean bowl and place a piece of wax paper or plastic wrap directly on the surface to prevent a skin from forming. Cool completely. Whisk in marshmallow creme and vanilla until as smooth as possible. (The mixture will be a little lumpy; the lumps will break down during stir-freezing.)

3. Pour into the canister of an ice cream maker and freeze according to the manufacturer's directions. If necessary, place the ice cream in the freezer to firm up before serving in chilled dessert dishes. (*Use within hours of freezing, if possible, or store in the freezer for up to 4 days. If the ice cream becomes very hard in the freezer, let it soften for 20 minutes before scooping.*)

Makes about 1½ quarts, serves 8.

240 calories per serving: 6 grams protein, 3 grams fat (1 gram saturated fat), 46 grams carbohydrate; 88 mg sodium; 85 mg cholesterol.

CINNAMON ICE CREAM

Serve a scoop of this subtly spiced ice cream with Caramelized Apple Topping (page 179) or on a wedge of New England Apple Pie (page 43).

1. In a large heavy saucepan, combine milk, brown sugar, cinnamon sticks and vanilla bean. Heat over medium heat, stirring to dissolve the sugar, until steaming. Remove from the heat, cover the pan and let steep for 30 minutes. Strain, discarding the cinnamon sticks and vanilla bean halves. (Scrape the tiny seeds inside the vanilla bean into the milk, if desired.)

2. In a mixing bowl, whisk together egg yolks, corn syrup, cornstarch and ground cinnamon. Gradually add the milk, whisking to combine, and return to the saucepan. Cook over medium heat, whisking constantly, until the mixture boils and thickens, about 3 minutes. (Because the custard is thickened with cornstarch, it will not curdle when it boils.)

3. Transfer the custard to a bowl and place a piece of wax paper or plastic wrap directly over the surface to prevent a skin from forming. Cover and refrigerate until no longer warm. Add marshmallow creme and mix with a whisk until as smooth as possible. (The mixture will be slightly lumpy, but will smooth out during stir-freezing.) Return to the refrigerator until completely chilled.

4. Pour the custard mixture into the canister of an ice cream maker and freeze according to the manufacturer's directions. If necessary, place the ice cream in the freezer to firm up before serving in chilled dessert dishes. (*Use within hours of freezing, if possible, or store in the freezer for up to 4 days. If the ice cream becomes very hard in the freezer, let it soften for 20 minutes before scooping.*)

Makes about 3 cups, serves 6.

255 calories per serving: 6 grams protein, 3 grams fat (1 gram saturated fat), 53 grams carbohydrate; 93 mg sodium; 76 mg cholesterol.

3 cups low-fat milk

2 tablespoons light brown sugar

6 cinnamon sticks, broken into small pieces

1 vanilla bean, split in half lengthwise

2 large egg yolks

¼ cup light corn syrup

2 tablespoons cornstarch

¼ teaspoon ground cinnamon

2 cups marshmallow creme, such as Fluff

◆**SUBSTITUTION**

If you don't have a vanilla bean, add 1 teaspoon pure vanilla extract to the milk after it has steeped.

MALT SHOP CHOCOLATE ICE CREAM

A favorite flavor from soda-shop days can now be had in a low-fat ice cream.

1½ teaspoons unflavored gelatin

2½ cups low-fat milk

1 14-ounce can nonfat sweetened condensed milk (*not* evaporated milk)

¼ cup unsweetened cocoa powder, preferably Dutch-process

½ cup malted-milk powder

¼ cup dark corn syrup

1 ounce unsweetened chocolate, coarsely chopped

1 teaspoon pure vanilla extract

1. In a small bowl, sprinkle gelatin over 1 tablespoon water; let stand until softened, 1 minute or longer.

2. In a heavy saucepan, combine ½ cup of the low-fat milk, sweetened condensed milk, cocoa, malted-milk powder and corn syrup; whisk until smooth. Bring to a simmer over medium heat, whisking constantly. Remove from the heat and add chocolate and the softened gelatin; stir until the chocolate has melted. Transfer the mixture to a bowl. Gradually whisk in the remaining 2 cups milk and vanilla until smooth. Chill until cold, about 1 hour.

3. Pour into the canister of an ice cream maker and freeze according to the manufacturer's directions. If necessary, place the ice cream in the freezer to firm up before serving in chilled dessert dishes. (*Use within hours of freezing, if possible, or store in the freezer for up to 4 days. If the ice cream becomes very hard in the freezer, let it soften for 20 minutes before scooping.*)

Makes about 1 quart, serves 6.

320 calories per serving: 11 grams protein, 5 grams fat (1 gram saturated fat), 60 grams carbohydrate; 149 mg sodium; 16 mg cholesterol.

◆**INGREDIENT NOTE**
Look for malted-milk powder between the instant cocoa and the nonfat dry milk on the supermarket shelf.

Malt Shop Chocolate Ice Cream

LEMON ICE CREAM

With a flavor reminiscent of lemon cheesecake, this easy-to-make ice cream is delicious sprinkled with fresh berries.

1	14-ounce can nonfat sweetened condensed milk
2	cups low-fat milk
⅔	cup fresh lemon juice
1	tablespoon grated lemon zest
⅛	teaspoon salt

In a mixing bowl, whisk together sweetened condensed milk, milk, lemon juice, lemon zest and salt. Freeze in an ice cream maker according to the manufacturer's directions. (*Alternatively, freeze the mixture in a shallow pan until solid, about 6 hours. Break into chunks and process in a food processor until smooth.*)

Makes about 1 quart, serves 6.

230 calories per serving: 8 grams protein, 1 gram fat (0.5 grams saturated fat), 47 grams carbohydrate; 154 mg sodium; 12 mg cholesterol.

WHITE GRAPE ICE

Serve garnished with frozen red grapes (page 165) and a lemon wedge for squeezing over the top.

½	cup sugar
4	cups seedless green grapes (about 2 pounds)
1½	cups chilled white grape juice

1. In a small saucepan, combine sugar and 1 cup water. Bring to a simmer and stir until the sugar is completely dissolved. Let the syrup cool to room temperature, then place it in the refrigerator to chill.

2. Set a shallow metal pan, such as a cake pan, in the freezer to chill. In a food processor or blender, puree grapes until smooth; strain into a large bowl, pressing firmly on the solids. Discard the solids. Add grape juice and the chilled sugar syrup to the puree; stir until well blended and pour into the chilled metal pan.

3. Place the pan in the freezer for 30 minutes, or until ice crystals form around the edges. Stir the ice crystals into the center of the pan and return to the freezer; repeat every 30 minutes, or until all of the liquid is frozen, about 3 hours.

4. To serve, scoop the ice into chilled bowls or goblets. If the ice has become too hard, scrape it with a large spoon to break up the crystals.

Makes about 5 cups, serves 6.

135 calories per serving: 1 gram protein, 0 grams fat, 36 grams carbohydrate; 3 mg sodium; 0 mg cholesterol.

ORANGE SORBET WITH MINTED ORANGES

If they are available, blood oranges are especially striking here.

TO MAKE SORBET:

Combine sugar, honey and ½ cup water in a small saucepan and bring to a boil. Reduce the heat to low and simmer for 10 minutes. Remove from the heat and allow to cool. Combine orange and lemon juices and sugar syrup in a large bowl. Freeze in an ice cream maker according to the manufacturer's directions. (*Alternatively, freeze the mixture in a shallow metal cake pan until solid, about 6 hours. Break into chunks and process in a food processor until smooth.*)

TO PREPARE ORANGES:

1. With a sharp knife, remove skin and white pith from oranges and discard. Working over a bowl to catch the juice, cut the orange sections from their surrounding membranes, discarding any seeds. Squeeze any juice from the membranes into the bowl; cover and refrigerate.

2. About 1 hour before serving, toss the oranges with orange liqueur and chopped mint. Refrigerate. If the sorbet has frozen solid, allow it to soften for about 30 minutes in the refrigerator before serving. To serve, scoop the sorbet onto individual dishes, spoon the oranges around it and garnish each dish with a sprig of mint.

Serves 6.

170 calories per serving: 2 grams protein, 0 grams fat, 40 grams carbohydrate, 1 gram alcohol; 4 mg sodium; 0 mg cholesterol.

SORBET

¼ cup light brown sugar

1 tablespoon mild-flavored honey

2½ cups fresh orange juice (about 10 oranges)

⅓ cup fresh lemon juice

MINTED ORANGES

6 navel *or* blood oranges

2-3 tablespoons Grand Marnier *or* other orange liqueur

2 tablespoons chopped fresh mint plus sprigs for garnish

Cran-Strawberry Ice Pops

CRAN-STRAWBERRY ICE POPS

These ruby-red frozen treats are bursting with fruit flavor.

2 cups fresh strawberries *or* frozen unsweetened strawberries, thawed

¼ cup frozen cranberry-juice concentrate, thawed

3 tablespoons sugar

1 tablespoon fresh lemon juice

In a blender or food processor, combine strawberries, cranberry-juice concentrate, sugar, lemon juice and 3 tablespoons water. Process until smooth. Pour the mixture into individual frozen-treat molds or small paper cups. Freeze for about 1 hour, or until beginning to set. Insert frozen-treat sticks and freeze until completely firm.

Makes eight 2-ounce pops.

35 calories per pop: 0 grams protein, 0 grams fat, 8 grams carbohydrate; 1 mg sodium; 0 mg cholesterol.

◆**SMART SHOPPER**

Most kitchenware stores sell frozen-treat molds and sticks throughout the summer; craft stores sell the sticks year-round.

FROZEN FUDGE BARS

Creamy, chocolaty and just like the ones from the corner store, but better.

In a heavy saucepan, whisk together sweetened condensed milk, sugar and cocoa until smooth. Stir the mixture with a wooden spoon over medium-low heat until it comes to a simmer; continue stirring for 1 minute. Very gradually, whisk in the low-fat milk, stirring to dissolve all the cocoa-sugar mixture. Remove the pan from the heat and stir in vanilla. Pour into individual frozen-treat molds or small paper cups. Freeze for abut 1 hour, or until beginning to set. Insert frozen-treat sticks and freeze until completely firm.

Makes eight 2-ounce bars.

120 calories per bar: 3 grams protein, 1 gram fat (0 grams saturated fat), 26 grams carbohydrate; 40 mg sodium; 4 mg cholesterol.

½ cup nonfat sweetened condensed milk

½ cup sugar

¼ cup unsweetened cocoa powder, preferably Dutch-process

1¼ cups low-fat milk

1 teaspoon pure vanilla extract

FROSTED GRAPES

Frozen grapes make a cool finish to hot, spicy meals.

Wash grapes and pat dry. Place in the freezer for 45 minutes. Remove from the freezer and let sit for 2 minutes before serving.

Serves 4.

105 calories per serving: 1 gram protein, 0 grams fat, 29 grams carbohydrate; 3 mg sodium; 0 mg cholesterol.

1½ pounds red or green seedless grapes

FROZEN YOGURT SANDWICHES

Great for the kids—or the kids at heart—frozen fruit swirled into frozen yogurt and sandwiched between two crisp oatmeal/whole-wheat cookies.

COOKIES

- ½ cup packed light brown sugar
- 2 tablespoons canola oil
- 1 tablespoon low-fat milk
- 1 large egg white
- 1 teaspoon pure vanilla extract
- 1 cup "quick" rolled oats
- ½ cup whole-wheat flour
- 1 teaspoon baking soda
- ½ teaspoon ground cinnamon

FROZEN YOGURT

- 2 cups frozen unsweetened fruit, such as cherries, blueberries, strawberries, peaches, slightly thawed
- 3 cups nonfat vanilla frozen yogurt

TO MAKE COOKIES:

1. Preheat oven to 300°F. Lightly oil 2 baking sheets or coat them with nonstick cooking spray; set aside.

2. In a mixing bowl, whisk together brown sugar, oil, milk, egg white and vanilla until no lumps of brown sugar remain. Add oats, flour, baking soda and cinnamon to the bowl and stir until no traces of dry ingredients remain.

3. Divide the dough into 16 equal pieces and form each piece into a ball. Place 8 balls on each prepared baking sheet. Cover each baking sheet with a piece of plastic wrap or wax paper; with a flat-bottomed cup or bowl, firmly press each of the balls into a thin 3-inch circle.

4. Bake the cookies, one sheet at a time, for 8 to 10 minutes, or until well-browned. Remove to a wire rack to cool completely.

TO FORM SANDWICHES:

If the pieces of fruit are large, coarsely chop them. Soften frozen yogurt in the microwave at medium-low power for 30 to 60 seconds or at room temperature for 10 to 20 minutes. In a mixing bowl, swirl the fruit into the softened frozen yogurt. If the yogurt has become too soft, return it to the freezer to firm up slightly. Scoop about ⅓ cup of frozen yogurt onto a cookie and gently press a second cookie on top. Repeat with the remaining cookies and frozen yogurt. Return the sandwiches to the freezer to firm up.

Makes 8 sandwiches.

280 calories per sandwich: 6 grams protein, 4 grams fat (0 grams saturated fat), 56 grams carbohydrate; 168 mg sodium; 0 mg cholesterol.

PEACH-MELON FROZEN YOGURT

If you start with frozen fruit and a food processor, you can have fat-free frozen yogurt in only 15 minutes.
Try frozen strawberries, blueberries or bananas, but avoid seedy fruits, such as raspberries.

In a food processor, combine frozen fruit and sugar. Pulse until coarsely chopped. In a small bowl, stir together yogurt and lemon juice. With the machine running, gradually pour the yogurt mixture through the feed tube. Process until smooth and creamy, scraping down the sides of the work bowl once or twice. Scoop the frozen yogurt into serving dishes, cover with plastic wrap and freeze for at least 15 to 30 minutes to firm up before serving.

Makes about 2½ cups, serves 4.

120 calories per serving: 3 grams protein, 0 grams fat, 29 grams carbohydrate; 62 mg sodium; 1 mg cholesterol.

- 3 cups frozen unsweetened mixed fruit, such as peaches, melon, grapes
- ⅓ cup sugar, preferably instant-dissolving
- ½ cup nonfat plain yogurt
- 1 tablespoon fresh lemon juice

BLUEBERRY-BANANA FROZEN YOGURT

Pureed banana gives this mixture an especially smooth texture, and orange-juice concentrate
and crème de cassis add a complementary tang.

In a food processor, puree blueberries. To remove skins, work the puree through a fine strainer into a bowl. Add bananas to the food processor and puree. Add the strained blueberry puree, yogurt, sugar, orange-juice concentrate and crème de cassis or black currant syrup and process just until mixed in. If necessary, chill until cold. Pour into the canister of an ice cream maker and freeze according to the manufacturer's directions. (*Alternatively, freeze the mixture in a shallow metal cake pan until solid, about 6 hours. Break into chunks and process in a food processor until smooth.*)

Makes about 1 quart, serves 6.

190 calories per serving: 3 grams protein, 1 gram fat (0 grams saturated fat), 44 grams carbohydrate, 1 gram alcohol; 36 mg sodium; 1 mg cholesterol.

- 1 quart blueberries
- ⅔ cup sliced ripe banana (1 medium)
- 1 cup nonfat plain yogurt
- ½ cup sugar, preferably instant-dissolving
- ¼ cup frozen orange-juice concentrate, thawed
- 1 tablespoon crème de cassis *or* black currant syrup

Raspberry Frozen Yogurt (*right*) & Sicilian Fig Cookies (*page 110*)

RASPBERRY FROZEN YOGURT

Keep raspberries on hand in the freezer year-round so you can make this luxurious, simple dessert anytime.

In a food processor, puree raspberries with lemon juice. To remove seeds, work the puree through a fine strainer into a bowl. Whisk in sugar and yogurt. If necessary, chill until cold. Pour into the canister of an ice cream maker and freeze according to the manufacturer's directions. (*Alternatively, freeze in a shallow metal cake pan or ice cube trays until solid, about 6 hours. Break into chunks and process in a food processor until smooth.*)

Makes about 1 quart, serves 6.

240 calories per serving: 3 grams protein, 1 gram fat (0 grams saturated fat), 60 grams carbohydrate; 30 mg sodium; 1 mg cholesterol.

3 pints raspberries

2 tablespoons fresh lemon juice

1⅓ cups sugar, preferably instant-dissolving

1 cup nonfat plain yogurt

MANGO-LIME SORBET

A stunning golden-orange color, this refreshing sorbet is even more dramatic served with Strawberry Margarita Sauce (page 174).

1. Puree mangoes in a food processor or blender. Work the puree through a fine sieve. (This will remove any fibers, the amount of which can vary.) Measure out 2 cups of puree, cover with plastic wrap and refrigerate (freeze any extra for another use).

2. In a saucepan, combine sugar and 1½ cups water. Stir over medium heat until the liquid comes to a full boil and the sugar has dissolved. Remove from the heat and let cool to room temperature. Stir in the reserved mango puree and lime juice, adding more lime juice if desired. Cover with plastic wrap and refrigerate until cold.

3. Freeze the mixture in an ice cream maker according to the manufacturer's directions. (*Alternatively, freeze the mixture in a shallow metal cake pan or ice cube trays until solid, about 6 hours. Break into chunks and process in a food processor until smooth.*)

Makes about 1 quart, serves 6.

270 calories per serving: 1 gram protein, 1 gram fat (0 grams saturated fat), 71 grams carbohydrate; 5 mg sodium; 0 mg cholesterol.

3 pounds ripe mangoes (3 large or 4 medium), peeled and cut into chunks (*see tip on page 59*)

1 cup sugar

¼ cup fresh lime juice, *or* more to taste

ORANGE SMOOTHIE

Like a Creamsicle in a glass.

1	cup nonfat vanilla frozen yogurt
¾	cup low-fat milk
¼	cup frozen orange-juice concentrate

Combine frozen yogurt, milk and orange-juice concentrate in a blender and blend until smooth.

Makes 2 cups.

185 calories per cup: 7 grams protein, 1 gram fat (1 gram saturated fat), 36 grams carbohydrate; 117 mg sodium; 4 mg cholesterol.

STRAWBERRY MALTED

Picture this in a chrome holder set on a marble counter.

1	cup fresh strawberry halves
1	cup nonfat vanilla frozen yogurt
⅔	cup low-fat milk
3	tablespoons malted-milk powder

Combine strawberries, frozen yogurt, milk and malted-milk powder in a blender and blend until smooth.

Makes 2 cups.

180 calories per cup: 7 grams protein, 2 grams fat (1 gram saturated fat), 33 grams carbohydrate; 133 mg sodium; 7 mg cholesterol.

MINTED LIME *LIQUADO*

A bright-green cooler inspired by the light fruit-and-ice shakes of Mexico.

¼	cup frozen limeade concentrate
¼	cup fresh mint leaves
5-6	ice cubes

Combine 1 cup water, limeade, mint and ice cubes in a blender and blend until smooth.

Makes 2 cups.

110 calories per cup: 0 grams protein, 0 grams fat, 29 grams carbohydrate; 7 mg sodium; 0 mg cholesterol.

Orange Smoothie

PRUNES & ARMAGNAC IN FROZEN YOGURT

The pairing of prunes and Armagnac is common in southwest France. The fruit is plumped in the brandy, then folded into frozen yogurt for a simple but glorious dessert.

½ cup chopped pitted prunes

3 tablespoons Armagnac *or* Cognac

3 cups nonfat vanilla frozen yogurt

1. In a saucepan, combine prunes and Armagnac or Cognac and stir over low heat until the prunes are softened, about 1 minute. Transfer the prunes to a bowl to cool down.

2. Soften frozen yogurt in the microwave at medium-low power (30 percent) for 30 to 60 seconds. (*Alternatively, allow the frozen yogurt to soften for 10 to 20 minutes at room temperature.*) Transfer to a bowl and stir in the prunes and any liquid with a wooden spoon or whisk until well incorporated. Return to the freezer until firm, about 2 hours.

Makes about 3½ cups, serves 4.

250 calories per serving: 5 grams protein, 0 grams fat, 44 grams carbohydrate, 4 grams alcohol; 106 mg sodium; 0 mg cholesterol.

◆**FLAVOR BOOSTERS**

Nonfat or low-fat vanilla frozen yogurt is a bit bland all on its own, but a wonderful base for flavoring in myriad ways. Try adding chopped fruits, ground spices or liqueurs, alone or in combination.

SUBLIME SAUCES

A solitary scoop of ice cream or frozen yogurt makes a rather ordinary dessert. But put a little Blackberry Sauce or Praline Sauce or Passion Fruit Sauce on top, and it is transformed. Yet it's hardly any work at all.

Many of these sauces are based on seasonal fresh fruits. The sweet intensity of tropical fruits is particularly useful in dessert sauces. Quite a few of these recipes contain spirits or wine, which is an efficient way to enhance flavors without adding any fat. If you prefer not to use alcohol, it can be omitted or substituted by an equal amount of fruit juice plus a little vanilla extract for complexity.

BLACKBERRY SAUCE

An uncooked sauce with a lovely blackberry flavor; delightful over Lemon Ice Cream (page 162).

3 cups blackberries

2 tablespoons blackberry brandy

2 tablespoons fresh orange juice

3 tablespoons honey

Pick over and reserve 1 cup of the smallest and most attractive berries. In a food processor, puree the remaining 2 cups berries with the brandy, orange juice and honey. Transfer the mixture to a sieve set over a bowl. Press the puree through the sieve and discard the seeds. (*The sauce can be made up to 8 hours ahead and stored, covered, in the refrigerator.*) Stir the remaining berries into the sauce just before serving.

Makes about 2 cups.

15 calories per tablespoon: 0 grams protein, 0 grams fat, 4 grams carbohydrate, 2 grams alcohol; 1 mg sodium; 0 mg cholesterol.

STRAWBERRY MARGARITA SAUCE

Serve this spirited sauce over Mango-Lime Sorbet (page 169) or fresh fruit.

12 ounces frozen unsweetened strawberries, thawed, *or* 4 cups fresh strawberries, hulled

½ cup confectioners' sugar

¼ cup fresh lime juice, *or* more to taste

2 tablespoons tequila

1 tablespoon Triple Sec *or* other orange liqueur

In a blender, combine strawberries, sugar, lime juice, tequila and liqueur. Blend on medium speed until smooth. Add more lime juice if desired.

Makes about 2 cups.

25 calories per tablespoon: 0 grams protein, 0 grams fat, 5 grams carbohydrate, 1 gram alcohol; 0 mg sodium; 0 mg cholesterol.

MEXICAN CHOCOLATE SAUCE

Chocolate syrup makes a quick base for a delicious sauce; cocoa powder deepens the chocolate flavor and cuts the sweetness without adding fat, and orange and cinnamon lend complexity.

In a small saucepan, stir together cocoa, cornstarch and cinnamon. Whisk in orange juice and zest and stir over medium-low heat until simmering and thickened. Add chocolate syrup and stir until the sauce is heated through. Serve warm over frozen yogurt. (*The sauce can be stored, covered, in the refrigerator for up to 1 week.*)

Makes 1½ cups.

35 calories per tablespoon: 0 grams protein, 0 grams fat, 10 grams carbohydrate; 8 mg sodium; 0 mg cholesterol.

¼	cup unsweetened cocoa powder, preferably Dutch-process
½	teaspoon cornstarch
¼	teaspoon ground cinnamon
½	cup fresh orange juice
1	teaspoon grated orange zest
1	cup chocolate syrup, such as Hershey's

COFFEE-RUM SAUCE

Sliced bananas make a delicious addition to this smooth, rich and intense sauce.

In a small bowl, whisk instant coffee and rum until the coffee dissolves (small flecks of undissolved coffee will remain). Whisk in sweetened condensed milk until well combined. Serve over frozen yogurt. (*The sauce can be stored, covered, in the refrigerator for up to 1 week.*)

Makes 1⅓ cups.

60 calories per tablespoon: 2 grams protein, 0 grams fat, 12 grams carbohydrate; 20 mg sodium; 2 mg cholesterol.

3	tablespoons instant coffee powder *or* granules
2	tablespoons dark rum
1	14-ounce can nonfat sweetened condensed milk

APRICOT-GINGERSNAP SAUCE

Colorful, tart and crunchy.

¾ cup fresh orange juice

½ cup slivered dried apricots

1 tablespoon brandy (optional)

¼ cup orange marmalade

4 gingersnaps, crushed

In a small saucepan, simmer orange juice, apricots and brandy, if using, over low heat until the apricots are soft, about 3 minutes. Add marmalade, increase the heat to medium-high and cook, stirring, until the sauce is slightly thick, about 5 minutes. Serve warm over frozen yogurt, sprinkled with crushed gingersnaps.

Makes 1 cup of sauce.

145 calories per ¼-cup serving: 1 gram protein, 1 gram fat (0 grams saturated fat), 34 grams carbohydrate; 47 mg sodium; 0 mg cholesterol.

WARM LEMON & GINGER SAUCE

A final fillip for simple poached pears or a slice of Buttermilk Pound Cake (page 23).

⅓ cup sugar

1 tablespoon cornstarch

¼ teaspoon ground cinnamon

¼ teaspoon ground ginger
   Pinch of salt

½ cup apple juice

¼ cup fresh lemon juice

1 tablespoon grated lemon zest

2 tablespoons finely slivered crystallized ginger

In a small saucepan, whisk together sugar, cornstarch, cinnamon, ground ginger and salt until completely blended. Slowly whisk in apple juice and ½ cup water. Whisk over medium heat until the sauce is simmering and thickened. Cook, stirring occasionally, until the sauce has thickened further, about 5 more minutes. Remove from the heat and stir in lemon juice, lemon zest and crystallized ginger. Serve warm.

Makes 1¼ cups.

20 calories per tablespoon: 0 grams protein, 0 grams fat, 5 grams carbohydrate; 1 mg sodium; 0 mg cholesterol.

♦**INGREDIENT NOTE**

Crystallized ginger lends a peppery pizzazz to desserts.
Buy it at Asian markets or health-food stores, where it will be far less expensive.

Praline Sauce on Vanilla Ice Cream (*page 158*)

PRALINE SAUCE

A saucy version of the Louisiana confection; add a splash of bourbon if you like.

1. In a small saucepan, melt butter over medium heat. Add pecans and stir until the nuts are lightly toasted and fragrant, about 1 minute. Remove the pan from the heat; stir in brown sugar.

2. In a small bowl, stir milk, cornstarch and salt together; whisk into the brown-sugar mixture. Return to the heat and whisk until the sauce is simmering and thick, about 1 minute. Serve warm over frozen yogurt.

Makes 1 cup.

70 calories per tablespoon: 0 grams protein, 2 grams fat (1 gram saturated fat), 14 grams carbohydrate; 12 mg sodium; 1 mg cholesterol.

2	teaspoons butter
¼	cup chopped pecans
1	cup packed dark brown sugar
⅓	cup low-fat milk
1	tablespoon cornstarch
	Pinch of salt

RASPBERRY-CHOCOLATE SAUCE

Raspberry jam adds sheen and a fruity accent to this scrumptious sauce.

⅓ cup sugar

2 tablespoons unsweetened cocoa powder

1 teaspoon arrowroot *or* 1½ teaspoons cornstarch

3 tablespoons seedless raspberry jam

2 teaspoons eau-de-vie de framboise *or* Chambord (optional)

In a small saucepan, whisk together sugar, cocoa and arrowroot or cornstarch. Gradually whisk in ¼ cup water and jam. Bring to a simmer over medium heat, whisking constantly. Remove from the heat and stir in liqueur, if using. Let cool slightly. (*The sauce can be stored, covered, in the refrigerator for up to 1 week.*)

Makes ⅔ cup.

40 calories per tablespoon: 0 grams protein, 0 grams fat, 10 grams carbohydrate; 1 mg sodium; 0 mg cholesterol.

CRAN-RASPBERRY SAUCE

Fruit juice is the base of this quick sauce that pairs well with fresh fruit, frozen yogurt or a slice of pound cake.

2 cups cranberry-raspberry juice

2 tablespoons kirsch *or* orange liqueur *or* 1 tablespoon water

1 teaspoon cornstarch

1 cup frozen unsweetened raspberries (*not* thawed)

In a large saucepan or skillet, bring juice to a boil over high heat. Cook until reduced to about ⅔ cup, about 10 minutes. In a small bowl, stir together kirsch, orange liqueur or water and cornstarch; whisk into the sauce and cook until it has thickened and become clear again. Remove the pan from the heat and stir in raspberries; let stand briefly until the berries have thawed. Serve warm or cool.

Makes 1 cup.

30 calories per tablespoon: 0 grams protein, 0 grams fat, 6 grams carbohydrate; 1 mg sodium; 0 mg cholesterol.

CARAMELIZED APPLE TOPPING

Simmered in caramel syrup, the apples soften and take on an amber translucence; spoon some over Cinnamon Ice Cream (page 159) or alongside Triple Gingerbread (page 26).

1. In a bowl, toss together apples and lemon juice; set aside.

2. In a heavy skillet, stir together sugar and 2 tablespoons water; bring to a boil, stirring to dissolve the sugar. Reduce the heat to low and cook, not stirring but swirling the pan, until the sugar turns a deep amber, about 5 minutes (if the sugar crystallizes, it will take longer, but will eventually melt and caramelize).

3. Remove the pan from the heat and swirl in butter. Transfer the apples to the pan, cover and return to low heat. Cook, stirring occasionally, until the caramel has dissolved and the apples are translucent, about 10 minutes. If using, stir in Calvados. Serve warm.

Makes about 1½ cups, serves 4.

210 calories per serving: 0 grams protein, 2 grams fat (1 gram saturated fat), 49 grams carbohydrate; 20 mg sodium; 5 mg cholesterol.

4	cooking apples, such as Cortland, Golden Delicious *or* Rome Beauty, peeled, cored and thinly sliced (4 cups)
1	tablespoon fresh lemon juice
⅔	cup sugar
2	teaspoons butter
1	tablespoon Calvados (*see page 10*), optional

BRANDIED CHERRY SAUCE

Try pairing this with a scoop of Malt Shop Chocolate Ice Cream (page 160).

In a saucepan, combine cherries, sugar and lemon juice. Bring to a simmer and cook, stirring, until the cherries have softened and exuded their liquid, about 5 minutes. In a small bowl, stir together brandy or orange juice and cornstarch. Stir the cornstarch mixture into the simmering liquid and cook until thickened and clear. Serve warm.

Makes about 1½ cups, serves 4.

190 calories per serving: 2 grams protein, 0 grams fat, 41 grams carbohydrate, 3 grams alcohol; 0 mg sodium; 0 mg cholesterol.

3	cups frozen dark sweet cherries
2	tablespoons sugar
1	tablespoon fresh lemon juice
2	tablespoons brandy *or* orange juice
1½	teaspoons cornstarch

SANGRIA SAUCE

Serve this over vanilla or peach frozen yogurt for a Sangria Sundae.

1   cup red wine

⅓   cup orange marmalade

4   clementines *or* tangerines,
    peeled, segmented and cut
    in half

1   teaspoon fresh lime juice

In a small saucepan, bring wine to a boil over medium-high heat. Cook until reduced to ¼ cup, 6 to 8 minutes. Add marmalade and cook until thickened, 1 to 2 minutes. Remove from the heat and stir in clementines or tangerines and lime juice. Serve warm or cold.

Makes about 1½ cups, serves 4.

110 calories per serving: 1 gram protein, 0 grams fat, 28 grams carbohydrate; 4 mg sodium; 0 mg cholesterol.

Sangria Sauce on Vanilla Ice Cream (*page 158*)

PINEAPPLE-MANGO TOPPING

If you have the time, toast some shredded coconut to sprinkle on top.

In a small bowl, combine pineapple, mango, brown sugar, lime juice and lime zest. Stir until the sugar dissolves. Serve over sorbet or frozen yogurt, garnished with mint sprigs if desired.

Makes 2 cups.

80 calories per ½-cup serving: 0 grams protein, 0 grams fat, 21 grams carbohydrate; 4 mg sodium; 0 mg cholesterol.

1	cup chopped fresh pineapple (¼ of a medium pineapple)
1	small mango, chopped (*see tip on page 59*)
2	tablespoons brown sugar
1½	tablespoons fresh lime juice
½	teaspoon grated lime zest
	Fresh mint sprigs for garnish (optional)

PASSION FRUIT SAUCE

Passion fruit provides concentrated tropical flavoring power, one that enhances the tastes of other fruits. Stir up this simple sauce to transform all kinds of soft fruit, such as mango, papaya, melon, strawberries, blueberries or raspberries.

Cut tops from passion fruits and scrape out all pulp into the bowl of a food processor. Process the pulp until liquefied, then strain through a sieve set over a bowl to remove the seeds. (*Alternatively, work the pulp through a sieve, pressing hard with the back of a spoon to separate the pulp from the seeds.*) Blend the juice with honey and citrus juice to taste, and rum if desired. Chill before serving. (*The sauce will keep up to 2 days in the refrigerator.*)

Makes 1 cup.

20 calories per tablespoon: 0 grams protein, 0 grams fat, 5 grams carbohydrate; 2 mg sodium; 0 mg cholesterol.

6	passion fruits
3	tablespoons honey, plus more to taste
	Fresh lime juice *or* lemon juice
2-3	tablespoons light rum (optional)

◆**CHOOSING PASSION FRUIT**
Buy fruits that feel relatively heavy. A wrinkled exterior signals ripeness.

VANILLA CUSTARD SAUCE

A lighter version of crème anglaise, *this sauce is thickened with egg whites as well as yolks, so watch it carefully to avoid curdling. Serve with poached fruits or simple desserts, such as Cranberry Baked Apples (page 64).*

½ vanilla bean, split lengthwise but left attached at one end, *or* 1 teaspoon pure vanilla extract

1¼ cups low-fat milk

3 tablespoons sugar

1 large egg

1. If using vanilla bean, combine it with milk in a small saucepan; bring nearly to a boil, stirring to avoid scorching on the bottom of the pan. Remove the pan from the heat, cover and set aside to steep for 30 minutes. (Omit this step if you are using extract; it is added later.)

2. Set a fine strainer over a bowl and reserve. In a heavy saucepan, heat the milk or vanilla milk to a simmer. In a bowl, whisk together sugar and egg until smooth; gradually whisk in a little of the hot milk to warm the egg. Pour the egg mixture back into the hot milk. Stir the custard constantly over low heat until it thickens enough to coat the back of a spoon evenly, about 7 to 8 minutes. Do not allow the sauce to boil, or it will curdle.

3. Immediately pour the custard through the strainer. Scrape the seeds of the vanilla bean into the custard, or add the extract. Cover with plastic wrap and refrigerate until chilled. (*The sauce can be stored, covered, in the refrigerator for up to 2 days.*)

Makes 1¼ cups.

15 calories per tablespoon: 1 gram protein, 0.5 grams fat (0 grams saturated fat), 3 grams carbohydrate; 11 mg sodium; 11 mg cholesterol.

VANILLA CREAM

This easy topping makes a great lower-fat stand-in for whipped cream.

1½ cups low-fat vanilla yogurt

½ cup light whipping cream

1 tablespoon confectioners' sugar

1 tablespoon Grand Marnier *or* other orange liqueur (optional)

1. Line a sieve with cheesecloth and set it over a bowl. (*Alternatively, use a coffee filter lined with filter paper.*) Spoon in yogurt and let it drain in the refrigerator until reduced to 1 cup, about 1 hour.

2. In a chilled mixing bowl with chilled beaters, whip cream to soft peaks. Add the drained yogurt, sugar and liqueur, if using; fold gently to mix. Serve immediately or refrigerate, covered, for up to 8 hours.

Makes about 2 cups.

20 calories per tablespoon: 1 gram protein, 1 gram fat (1 gram saturated fat), 1 gram carbohydrate; 9 mg sodium; 4 mg cholesterol.

RECIPE INDEX

Page numbers in italics indicate photographs

LOWEST OF THE LOW

While all the recipes in this book can be considered low-fat, 41 recipes stand out as being particularly low in fat and 29 have no fat at all.

VERY LOW-FAT

(1, 2 or 3 grams of fat per serving)

NONFAT

CREDITS

Our thanks to the fine food writers whose work was previously published in EATING WELL *Magazine.*

Nancy Baggett:
Brandied Cherry Sauce, 179.

Melanie Barnard:
Banana Spice Cake, 19; Triple Gingerbread, 26; Mixed-Berry Champagne Ambrosia, 52; Tropical Fruit Compote, 59; Huckleberry Slump, 75; Summer Pudding, 76; Sicilian Fig Cookies, 110; Peppered Lebkuchen, 114; Mexican Meringue Cookies, 126; Blackberry Sauce, 174.

Melanie Barnard & Elinor Klivans:
A Bowl-of-Fruit Cake, 14.

Nora Carey:
Candied Grapefruit Peels, 68.

Lisa Cherkasky:
Rhubarb Custard Pie, 32.

Susan Herrmann Loomis:
Provençal Pear Tart, 46. (This recipe also appears in *The French Farmhouse Cookbook*; Workman, 1996.)

Joan Nathan:
Dried Fruit Compote, 63.

Bill Neal:
Peaches & Dumplings, 71.

Mäni Niall:
Blackberry Skillet Cake, 17; Pear Frangipane, 54; Cranberry-Walnut Scones, 143.

Marie Piraino:
Poppy Seed-Orange Biscotti, 120.

Susan G. Purdy:
Ricotta Cheesecake, 12; Orange Chiffon Cake, 24; Café au Lait Cheesecake, 30; Two-Berry Pie, 33; Chocolate Soufflé, 94; Cocoa Roulade with Raspberry Cream, 98; Spiced Coffee Cake with Pears, 145; Blueberry Coffee Cake, 146; Prune Coffee Cake, 147; Orange Marmalade Coffee Cake, 148. (These recipes also appear in *Have Your Cake & Eat It, Too* by Susan G. Purdy; William Morrow & Company, Inc., 1993.)

Stephan Pyles:
Mango-Cranberry Cobbler, 90.

Richard Sax:
Upside-Down Apple Pie, 41; Spiced Wine & Fruit, 63; Souffléed Semolina Pudding, 84; Apricot Fool, 88; Vanilla Custard Sauce, 182.

Elizabeth Schneider:
Passion Fruit Sauce, 181.

Michele Scicolone:
Italian Cornmeal Cake, 29; Apples Poached in White Wine, 62; Baked Rice Pudding, 82; Pine Nut Cookies, 111; Hazelnut-Anise Biscotti, 118; White Grape Ice, 162.

Martha Rose Shulman:
Orange Sorbet with Minted Oranges, 163.

Andrew Silva:
Sangria Sauce, 180.

Lucia Watson:
Chocolate Angel Food Cake, 102.

John Willoughby & Chris Schlesinger:
Roasted Pineapple, 55.

More cookbooks
from

EATING WELL
BOOKS

The Eating Well New Favorites Cookbook

More Great Recipes from the Magazine of Food & Health

From the Editors of EATING WELL®

ISBN 1-884943-07-1 (hardcover) $24.95 / ISBN 1-884943-08-X (paperback) $16.95

The Eating Well Rush Hour Cookbook

Healthy Meals for Busy Cooks

From the Editors of EATING WELL® The Magazine of Food & Health

ISBN 1-884943-05-5 (hardcover) $24.95 / ISBN 1-884943-06-3 (paperback) $14.95

The Eating Well Recipe Rescue Cookbook

High-Fat Favorites Transformed Into Healthy Low-Fat Favorites

Edited by Patricia Jamieson & Cheryl Dorschner

ISBN 1-884943-00-4 (hardcover) $24.95 / ISBN 1-884943-01-2 (paperback) $15.95

The Eating Well Cookbook

A Deluxe Collection of EATING WELL's Finest Recipes

Edited by Rux Martin, Patricia Jamieson & Elizabeth Hiser

ISBN 1-884943-02-0 (hardcover) $24.95 / ISBN 1-884943-03-9 (paperback) $15.95